They Serve Bagels in Heaven

One couple's story of love, eternity, and the cosmic
importance of everyday life

Irene Weinberg

ISBN-10: 1493618660
- EAN-13: 9781493618668

Dedication

I would like to dedicate this book with much love to my wonderful role model, my mother Thelma Stein (Temmy). Mom's loving, often humorous perspectives, her exceptional open- mindedness, her admirable ability to adjust, adjust, adjust, and her deep inner wisdom are true Blessings in my life.

Acknowledgments

This book is a revised edition of my original book titled <u>Love's Eternal Marriage: Bridging Heaven and Earth</u>. In that edition I acknowledged the many wonderful family members and friends whose love, help, faith, encouragement and support were there for me at any point during the writing of that book.

This time around, I want to welcome and acknowledge three very special and precious young boys who are tremendous Blessings to all of us who know them: my grandsons Noah Charlie Zall and David Simon Zall and my step-grandson Skye Andrew Weinberg.

I am also eternally grateful for seven "angels" in my life whose contributions, personal or pragmatic, were integral to the completion of this newly revised book:

Dr. Ange DiBenedetto's smart coaching and faith in me has never wavered, continuing to keep me grounded and moving forward. Seta Araz Shahinian's luminous faith and healing gifts, which have been a guiding light in my life, helped me illuminate both the personal and spiritual truths in the new last chapter of this book. My mom, the inimitable and wonderful Temmy, contributed very insightful and smart edits to my new last chapter as did my friends Marisa Bolognese and Laura Quinn, whose constructive editing ideas were also very helpful. And to my "sister" Carolyn Parrs, whose prescient embrace of Spirituality preceded and later validated mine, I thank you for your constant friendship and support.

I call my seventh angel my "Computer Angel," because both the original book and this newly revised edition would not exist without Michael Kida's incredible technical expertise and generosity of spirit. *I am grateful to each of you from the bottom of my heart!*

Who shall live for the sake of others,
Who, dying, shall leave a heritage of life.
—*New Union Prayer Book for the Days of Awe*

"Saul has to go. Many lessons will be learned from his death."

Saul and I were in our house on a lovely fall Sunday afternoon. He was watching football in the den while I washed dishes in the kitchen, some classical music on low in the background. Those words were so clear, and so clearly being spoken to me, that I actually turned to look behind me to see if someone had come into the room. There was no one else there.

I went into the den to bring Saul a glass of water. Standing behind him, I kissed the top of his head and pressed my cheek against his soft, red beard. We watched the game together that way for a few minutes. I took a deep breath in an effort to push away those words that had forced themselves into my mind, but it was hard to ignore that somebody somewhere was telling me I might lose the love of my life.

A few months later, that's just what happened.

It was the week before Christmas, and we were finally able to escape to our ski house in the Catskills. It had always been a sanctuary for both of us, and Saul badly needed a break after suffering through a grueling month of business upsets. His recent bone weariness scared me—the pain was much more intense for him this time. Other business upsets had bothered him, but this seemed to be seriously wounding him. It was so different that I feared he was heading into a decline over the endless work and the deep frustrations and disappointments he seemed to face every day now. It may have been the fact that the message had warned me of an enormous change to come; I'm not sure. Whatever the reason, I must have known this might have been his time to go. Because of all that, I was determined to make this *his* weekend.

And it was great. We went to all the restaurants he loved, we skied on his favorite slopes, and we spent time with dear friends. We even made love in the hot tub. He too must have sensed something because afterward, he held me close and said, "I'm so lucky and thankful to have you in my life."

On the way home the next day, he fell asleep at the wheel. As I felt the car go into a swerve, I cried out, "Saul!" Hearing me, he picked his head up off his chest and, with an unnatural calm, tried to right the car. As he turned the wheel, the car swerved so sharply in the middle of the road that we became airborne. Just before it flipped over, I heard these words reverberate within and around me:

"He's not going to make it. You are."

Somehow, I was in a state of total acceptance. There was something about these words, along with the other message, that gave me strength. Shock may have had something to do with it too, I suppose, but I don't think shock alone would've kept me that calm. When we landed, the car slammed down hard, turning and hitting four more times before rolling down a steep embankment. It was totaled. When we finally stopped, I looked at Saul and knew all through me that he was dead.

He was gone, while I survived. Saul's beautiful, outrageous spirit was no longer in his body. His warm, strong arms, his intelligent blue eyes, and his big, gorgeous heart were all lifeless now.

Even though I hadn't died, my injuries were so severe that I wondered how much longer I might be alive. Something had happened to my right eye—it felt like it was on fire. My collarbone had totally reversed itself, and the bone of my shoulder, which had sustained the strongest blows, had pushed so far out of my skin that it felt like I'd sprouted an angel wing. Worst of all, a jagged piece of metal had pierced an artery in my foot so deeply that I was hemorrhaging.

As I started trying to help myself, I felt the car being turned over.

Next, the two strong arms of an EMT were reaching in through my broken window, grabbing me by the shoulders, and beginning to pull me out. It was then that I heard a third and final message that confirmed the other two messages for me beyond any doubt. This one I just *knew* was the voice of God, our true source, saying to me:

"Be loving and kind to everyone."

I had just lost the love of my life. I was battered, cold, and bleeding profusely, but these words managed to fill me with love, compassion, and a profound knowing. I knew I was being given a directive from heaven itself. Whatever lay ahead, I knew I could accomplish it with as much love and kindness as possible (under the circumstances, anyway). I also knew without a doubt that I wasn't alone, which was a good thing because the business and family troubles I had waiting for me would have weakened an ox.

Saul and I had each begun a journey that would take us on different paths we needed to walk—still together somehow, even though I was now very much alone.

Saul's Journey

Hi. My name is Saul Weinberg and I'd like to share my story with you.

Sounds like an AA meeting, doesn't it? Except instead of a journey to sobriety, I'm telling a modern-age, sacred allegory that's packed with seeds of eternal truth and neatly wrapped up in an easy-to-read label.

The one thing I want to make straight from the start is this: I am not here to create a new theology. My story is simply *my* experience of the truth. All I know is what I've been through, and all I want to do is share it with you. As for calling it a story, well, let's face it: human beings live and learn by telling and sharing stories. Always have, probably always will. The only difference here is I'm telling mine from a place that offers me a vast, compassionate perspective. That's my job. Your job, if you want it, is to take whatever wisdom you can get from my tale and allow that light to nourish the beliefs about life and heaven you already have. I just hope that reading about my timeless love for Irene might help you find the inspiration you need to start living love as a practical behavior.

All right, already. Enough prefacing. On with the story! Let's start with my crossing over from Earth to heaven.

On December 21, 1997, I fell asleep at the wheel of my car. My beloved Irene was seated beside me. By the grace of God, she was spared, but I died and crossed over. I guess that fact in some ways makes this a travel story, because it *does* center on the journey I took from one plane of existence to another. But to me this is really a love story, because the love Irene and I share was and is so strong, and so true, that it lived on beyond my physical earthly being. That is some love, let me tell you.

I'll never forget the first time I saw my Irene. She stopped me in my tracks with a wallop that wasn't just physical desire—it was more like a direct hit to my gut. I knew that in this woman I'd found a force that could change my life. This moment took me, a young(ish), driven, sexually frustrated Jewish businessman, out of a lack of personal awareness I'd had no idea I was in. There was a truth in what I saw in Irene that showed me how, before her, I had been living life like an empty game. Just like that, in a moment -- all that truth wrapped up in the tilt of her face…and that cute little ass of hers. In that one moment, I became committed to finding a way through the protective shell of this shy, overly structured housewife. I could sense that just beneath the surface of her careful exterior lurked a volcanic core of passion. Once I took *that* first step, it was all over, boy. I was in love.

What I didn't understand back then was that in trying to reach her, I was also trying to reach out to myself. For me the keenest switch to the heart of our passion came from how Irene's generous, overflowing love called forth the best parts of me—parts I had never met before.

I could go on and on about this woman, but I'll spare you for now. I just want to give you one more essential piece of the whole before going any further. It has to do with a perspective I gained from the journey I took after my physical death—a broader, more compassionate perspective that's all about the incredible value of living and of loving.

Here's the deal: I didn't know how great life was while I was in the middle of it. Quite the opposite, in fact. Ask Irene today, and she'll tell you stories about a middle-aged man who, in a bunch of ways, turned from the love she was offering; a man who got swallowed whole by his real estate business. About a guy who appeared warm, funny, and kind to the outside world but who, deep down, remained aloof and unfed. I never cut myself enough slack to love myself first—and then those around me—fully.

But now I know, God damn it, just when it might be too late to do anything about it. After all, love is best expressed through the eyes and hands, the arms and skin, and, above all, the voice. And here I sit: all wisdom and no body, all thoughts and ideas bursting with love and no voice to carry them out.

What tops off my already huge regret like a giant red cherry is one more complexity I shut out while I was alive. I'm talking about infinite wisdom—that unknown mystery that weaves itself in and out of your life in the most unpredictable ways. I believe infinite wisdom was an integral part of my character and experiences on Earth. I believe that same infinite wisdom enables me to maintain my loving connection with Irene, to feel her heart and the love she feels for me even though I don't stand next to her anymore.

This new awareness of needing to live love and to stay more attuned to infinite wisdom came to me too late. I want my story to help you know these things while you still have a body to celebrate them with. It's why I've gone through all this trouble to communicate it to you in the first place. I truly hope that through the example of the love Irene and I share, you might be comforted, given strength, or in some way shown the many paths available for you to live more deeply and love more happily.

Without further ado, then, let me give you an inside view of what it's like to leave the earth plane and go into heaven.

I think my soul left even before my body died. The pain of living, especially over the last eight years, had become such a burden that this sudden moment filled me with profound relief. My last earthly recollection is driving, and then…this immense loosening and lightening.

For an instant, anyway. Then Irene called out my name, pulling me far enough back into my body so I could handle this accident in a way that made sure she lived through it. That was my final gut instinct: to steer the car so the accident would be the least destructive to her and to make sure that no one else would be harmed. I also knew in every fiber of my being this absolutely would be the last time I would hear her call my name.

After the accident, I left my body and was outside the car. From where I stood, I could see my body slumped over the steering wheel. Even though I knew something awful had happened to me, all I could focus on was Irene. Was she all right? Was she going to live?

As I looked around for help, I began to realize that while I was seeing, hearing, and thinking, I had *no body*. But there wasn't time to process this wacky thought because Irene was in mortal danger. If I had any faculties left at all, I was going to use them to help her.

Despite my concern, it dawned on me that my wife, the car, and the bare winter trees weren't all I could see. Surrounding Irene was a brilliant emerald and blue light that extended to the growing number of people who had stopped to help. It permeated each and every one of them with a magnificent purple light.

More than the beauty and wonder of this light was that it held within it angels—honest-to-God *angels*. In that instant, I understood they were there to protect us—all of us—before they helped me cross over. My knowing somehow came through the intensity of the radiance in which they held me. The warmth and strength of that radiance reassured me, helping me accept the fact that my life force, my bodiless soul, was now safely cocooned in love and light.

It's no easy thing, let me tell you, watching your death unfold before you. I missed the familiarity of my solid body so much it ached. But the power of the love beaming from my angels was complete and nourishing enough to anchor me while I tried to get used to my new situation. Their presence did ease the unbearable emptiness that engulfed me, but it was not strong enough to move my attention away from Irene. She was in trouble, and I couldn't help her; I couldn't do anything. My frustration twisted like an anchor searching for the ocean floor.

My angels steadied me as they showed me, in a devastating flash, all the hours and days, months, even years that lay ahead for Irene without me. I saw how she would long for me, call out my name, and sob for the comfort of being held in my arms. Just as this painful vision reached an almost unbearable crescendo, the angels allowed me to see the love Irene would receive from our family and friends as she grieved. I saw how she would eventually blossom into a new life without me and how, in the end, I would be there to greet her in heaven. Most importantly, I was allowed to see the literal, eternal soul bond Irene and I share. With its image before me, I could see why our love would never die, that that cord would keep us connected even all the way from Earth to heaven.

The reality of the depth and strength of my love for Irene began to warm me all over. This love connected me to the angelic light surrounding me. I didn't know it yet, but I would soon see how this newfound soul sensing of the power of love would begin turning me toward heaven—toward home. I found myself following my love for Irene, literally, as she was moved from the accident scene to the hospital. By keeping my focus on her and on the incredibly vivid memories of our family life together, I was actually able to move through time and space to continue my connection with my wife's heart as the hospital team worked to save her life. I watched the surgeon begin putting her back together. I watched my children as they waited down the hall for news. I watched in amazement as Irene modeled for me the eternal way love thrives and endures even as she fought for her life.

How can I explain this? She knew I was dead. She even turned to the doctor whose job it was to give her that bad news and comforted *him* while he told her the details of my death. In the face of all that, Irene still managed to share her gratitude for how wonderful our life together had been with the nurses and doctors who worked on her. The strength and love in her heart at those moments shot out from her core like a laser, upholding and protecting me as I made my crossing.

As they put her under anesthesia -- and I knew she was going to be all right -- I took in this gift, gathered myself, and said good-bye: to Irene, to my kids, to the air outside. When I did this, the walls of the hospital room and all the people inside it dissolved into darkness. I knew, with a deep and profound sadness, that I was also saying good-bye to life.

I turned my back and headed toward a vast portal I knew I had to enter. My strongest memory of this part of the journey is feeling intensely small and insignificant as I moved through this windy, dark vastness. I quickly realized the only thing that kept me from being lost in this darkness was embracing any skill of crying out for heavenly help I'd ever learned or stumbled upon in my lifetime. I faced the fear of this tremendous unknown by instinctively wrapping myself in every piece of the Torah I could recall. I also kept reviewing loving memories of Irene and the kids. I held on to my good Jewish prayers and Irene's love like two solid handrails above a shifting footbridge.

This was the void between heaven and Earth. I knew that now, and the only possible reaction to being there was to surrender to it completely. The moment I did that, I saw that famous white light and was carried toward it positively bathed in love. I surfaced as if from the bottom of a well into the light of heaven. The first thing I saw there was the warm, almost desperately happy, and unbelievably welcoming face of my mother, Belle...

Heaven

My mother was waiting for me with open arms. I hadn't seen her since she had died when I was sixteen, and I had missed her every day of my life. Now here she stood for me to hug and hold again. My angels let me see Belle as I remembered her from our life together. It took all the concentration she could muster to shape her soul fibers back into her old physical being, but she knew how necessary it was for me to have her there in a form I remembered. My wonderful, loving mom even managed to manifest her favorite housedress and hairdo just for me!

Belle was crying to beat the band, she was so happy to see me. She hadn't been ready to leave me and my brother Irv so early, and she'd spent a lot of anxious moments in heaven aware of the mistakes we were making and how we were being wounded by life, all without being able to be there in person to help. I could see how it also comforted and healed *her* to be able to spend this time with me now.

My mom was there to help me accept the reality of heaven so I didn't lose myself in a tailspin of disbelief. Seeing my mother as I'd known her, and being held within the light of her soul right then, meant the world to me.

The reason familiar touchstones such as these help a soul so much at this point is because, quite honestly, dying is as disorienting as all get-out. This process helps a soul release the memory of that cold, empty void that veils heaven from Earth. We pass through the void on the way to and from the earth plane each time we incarnate and die. The darkness of that place holds the potential for and mystery of all of life, and life is born from it, but it is *not* the coziest place to hang out in, I can tell you. Not to mention the fact that it takes some time to get used to not having a body, which made me feel naked, raw, and abandoned. Being held in Belle's love felt much better, much safer, much more familiar.

She held me in a soul embrace, a communion, really, of our conscious senses of each other's being. I have never had such a warm, accepting welcome, not anywhere. Her warmth and kindness steadied me, preparing me to meet my angels and stand before my loving Source.

After we'd hugged for what felt like forever, my angels led us to a deli where we had coffee and bagels. Imagine what a shock *that* was: to realize I had traveled God knows how far from the only life I could remember (at least to that point) only to discover that even up in heaven—hell, even without a body!—I could still get a cup of coffee and a bagel. Yes!

The memory of all the times I'd shared food with my mother steadied me further. I began to feel enough like my old self to start laughing with and teasing her the way I used to. She'd always been so serious, so worried about my father, who'd been a terror to live with because of his mental illness. That kind of teasing had always been a way for us to comfort each other. I felt deeply grateful for her help as I began to face another difficult passage.

After enjoying each other's company for a good while, my mom knew she'd done all she could to prepare me for the next step in my heavenly journey. She smiled warmly as she gave me over to the care of my angels.

I can't decide the best way to introduce you to the presence of – hell, even the *idea* of angels, so let me just jump right in. Angels are points of radiant consciousness whose concentrated love and compassion enable them to take personal shape when they're in the presence of a newly arriving soul like mine. To call them gorgeous is a major understatement. Nothing in my belief system on Earth had prepared me for the show-stopping glory of even one of these beings, let alone a host of them! Their faces held all the beauty of every race on Earth, and they smiled at me with a compassionate wisdom that ran as deep as the roots of the tallest California redwood. Enveloped in their radiating compassion, I began the jarring transition of returning from mortal being back to pure soul. No sooner had I adjusted to this than I found myself instantly, mysteriously standing before the Creator of all life. (And to think I once thought facing my accountant was tough!)

This point I cannot stress enough: there is *no* love and truth like this moment anywhere in the universe. I felt the pulse of the origin of life beating within and around me, holding me in a loving embrace that made me feel utterly accepted for being exactly as I was, as I am. The comfort of this acceptance moved me to pulse right along with the heartbeat of our loving Source. What a moment of truth that was—what a glorious thing to be in the presence of such profound truth. Not only is there glory, there is also a reawakening of one's own eternal wisdom.

Each soul that incarnates is given some degree of camouflage around its eternal knowledge—a sort of veil of forgetfulness, if you will. If you came to Earth without it, your constant awareness of heaven's love and glory would all but prevent you from living your human life. It's a delicate balancing act that's no longer necessary once the body is gone. When this transition takes place, your consciousness shifts from your identification with your body to identification with your soul and the eternal truths of what it means to be a living soul in heaven and on Earth. You then identify with these truths and begin understanding you have some healing, growing, and *celebrating* to do!

Standing with my Source in this throbbing cortex of crystalline light and pure sound, I could see the entire human race in all its tender craziness and heroic courage, all the way back to the very beginning. I could also see why there is a need for so many different religions on Earth. The beauty of our loving Source is so large and eternal that it takes a huge diversity of cultures and traditions to even come close to a full expression of the totality of our Creator. There is no one name, and there is no male or female to this immense entity: it is all things and all glory, and, most of all, it is *love*.

In this love, I could also see the tragedy of how people have often taken the original word of this divine presence and twisted it to shape practices that help them avoid spiritual growth rather than walk through it, or embrace it genuinely. Like when people believe it's okay to kill one another or persecute each other over religious differences. Or when they use prayer and meditation as ways to avoid strong emotions, let alone using religious tenets to dominate and destroy women.

But none of that dimmed the power of the beauty around me. Understand that, while I was alive as Saul Weinberg, I was a total skeptic about any notions of celestial beauty. Now, I know I can't convince any of you of the reality of this experience. It might even be impossible to imagine any of this until you die, cross over, and remember it all once you're brought back into this belongingness. But I have to give it a try because what I experienced next went beyond seeing visions or feeling love. It's not easy to describe since I don't have earthbound reference points to use for comparison, but I'm giving it a shot because it's the root of what I want to share with you.

Okay, here goes: When the soul stands with the Source of all life, there's an intimate connectedness so intense it feels like a living definition of interconnectedness itself. I could barely hold on to my hat within this onrush of ecstatic interchange. Every pulse of my soul core shifted with the rhythm of color and melody around me. Each response I had to everything immediately affected my environment. I was sure I'd be broken by the intensity of intermingling with all this light and sound. There with the Source, I began to see things in an entirely different way. This profound communion showed me how so much of what I had been attached to on Earth had never been the whole truth. As I settled into that realization, any final buffers left between me and the truth were removed. I was no longer capable of any forms of denial. All the reasons I'd ever used for choosing harsh or unloving behavior toward others or myself were suddenly meaningless.

With that denial stripped away, everything boiled down to one thing: acceptance. There's a lot a soul has to discover about acceptance, not the least of which is accepting that you *were* on Earth and you're now in heaven. There are also elements about remembering how you behaved in your last life that have to be worked through with incredible delicacy. That's partly why heavenly healing is unique to each individual. Mine was no exception. I had to be handled with kid gloves because it was too hard that early in my arrival for my soul to understand that I'd had a part in blocking help from heaven during my lifetime. It's one thing to see all the pain you ever experienced all at once. It's an even bigger shock to find out you had a part in keeping yourself in that pain.

In my defense, my blocking of heaven's help was not a conscious act. Most of the blocks came from having been burned so badly by all the pain I suffered every day in both work and life. It wasn't bad enough that I had been engulfed by all that suffering; I now had to see my part in stopping any help. Without knowing it, I'd put up a wall that totally shut out the loving energy God constantly sent my way. Every time I had embraced anger or resentment, had been judgmental, or had felt there was no good way out of a dark place, I'd left no room for heaven to enter and help me.

This is not to say my body, emotions, and needs on Earth hadn't needed to be tended to and cared for while I was alive. They had; they had been sacred. But now that all the denial was stripped away, my focus moved from the memory of those earthly needs and emotions to the core elements that remained. And these had nothing to do with social position, resources, who I was, or what I had or had not done. The light washing around and through me touched me with an understanding that life was really only about whether or not I had given and received love.

Without the burden (and blindness) inherent in denial and mere survival, the first thing I became aware of was any harm I had caused others and whether or not I had attempted atonement or reconciliation. Following right on the heels of that was a crystal-clear picture of all the times I'd allowed others to hurt me and the times I'd become lost in being treated as a victim. That was no picnic to relive, I can tell you, but my angels helped by offering a memory of love they hoped would help my consciousness open enough to move forward in my adjustment to heaven. They bathed me in a compassionate radiance, a kind of lilting melody that acknowledged all the acts of love I had engaged in every day on Earth. That's the way conversation seems to work up here—you get information as the energy of that shared, pulsing love washes over you. Man, the purity and sweetness of that love are incredible! It felt to me like the culmination of every beautiful piece of music I'd ever heard on Earth.

Through this I saw how every time I'd been kind to someone at the grocery store or been generous to others either financially or emotionally, the fabric of love that holds us all together had been strengthened. Heaven showed me right then and there that *this* is how each of us serves as the living eyes and presence of God every single day of our lives.

I knew in this moment with our Source that these are the core elements of life that truly matter. These fundamental acts and gestures revolve around giving and receiving love as a behavior -- which is way deeper than feeling love while still being able to hurt others or allowing yourself to be wounded.

Love is a behavior. It's something you feel in your heart and then live as a continual action. It is an action of respect for those around you, an action of loving them in a way that is easiest for them to receive it rather than what's easiest for you to give. Your first experiences in heaven are all geared toward helping you remember this truth about love.

Maybe an analogy will help you understand the way heaven communicates these lessons. The best one I can think of is a collage, some whole piece made up of a collection of images and themes. Take this idea and expand it into a collage made up of every religion's view of heaven, then mix that up with every single person's view of heaven. Finally mix in all the existing eternal truths about creation, love, sin, and salvation. That's heaven.

But remember: when you first get here, all you can see is your own belief about what heaven *should* be like. You have to be here for a good while before you can see under the layers of your own learned bias to find the real heaven. It's pretty intense, actually, and the truth is, if you didn't have some kind of filter -- especially when you first arrive, you would be overwhelmed by the kaleidoscope of color, sound, and form that goes on here.

Your filter is made up of the life and belief systems you embraced during the lifetime you're just coming back from. My filter was the Jewish-American culture. My new understanding of life and eternity soon softened these reference points. I then began my journey back to the full consciousness of eternal life.

After Belle helped me adjust and I met with my Creator, I was taken on a tour of heaven. This was done to help me decide where I wanted to heal and serve. At this point, I'd adjusted enough to eternal grace to be able to see the landscape through multi-generational and multi-cultural eyes, eternal eyes. Although what I'm sharing with you is colored by my personal bias, please understand that though there is great truth in what I'm saying, there is lots of room for the experiences of other souls and religions. There is no one person or culture who could ever adequately express the beauty and mystery of our loving Source's grace as it shines in heaven. In the face of it all, words are sketchy signposts at best, pointing awkwardly to larger truths that can be comprehended only by being lived through.

Having said that, let me give you a sense of what I saw and felt on my tour. It was like riding on a boat through the streets of Venice, being shown all the different neighborhoods that make up that old, historical city. I saw many, many neighborhoods in heaven, each dedicated to celebration and education in some diverse, unique way. It felt like I was floating past an eternal party, one where nobody was going to have a hangover since they were all drunk on love. I can't emphasize enough the intensity of the joy I saw on everyone's face. This joy is one of the universal, eternal facts of heaven. All souls see and feel this joy when they arrive, no matter what religious or cultural filter they are seeing it through.

When I say I saw people, or the faces of people, I mean each of the souls I encountered in heaven appeared to me in a form that is human-like. Their facial features are composites of all the lifetimes they'd lived. Whether a soul has lived only once or a thousand times, all the eternal characteristics of that being are energetically shaped to create an image that is a kind of holographic representation of a human being, only far more radiant. The composite is neither young nor old; it just, for lack of a better word, *is.*

I saw joyous children and joyous craftspeople. I was served coffee and cake by some of the happiest waiters you'll ever meet. I asked one of them, "How is it you came all the way to heaven and ended up as a waiter, yet you're so ridiculously happy?"

He laughed and said to me, "I'm happy because I also have time to work on perfecting my soul purpose, which is forestry. Everybody chooses to do some service in heaven that helps keep the fabric of a neighborhood intact. This is my neighborhood service, and I love it. But I also get time in the woods each day to study the perfect archetypal form of trees and what keeps them healthy. I get time to help record that information in heavenly records. I also have the fun of communing with the angels who make my knowledge available to any earthly foresters who are open to inspiration as they enjoy the beauty of the trees in their care."

"Sounds like heaven to me," I said. "But let me ask you one more thing. Doesn't all that work and creativity get a little lonely? Where does a person go for love and affection around here?"

My new friend had a good laugh over that one. "You get right to the point, don't you? Well," he continued, "the truth is that one of the main joys of heaven is what we learn here about how to give and receive love in any relationship. Everyone is given an abundance of opportunities every day to start and maintain healthy, lasting, intimate relationships and friendships, sisterhoods, and brotherhoods. That's the real heaven, man -- all that communing and giving and receiving is beyond ecstatic. It really helps you prepare for the much harder test of giving and receiving love under the stresses of being down on Earth."

Well, that gave me something to chew on. As I continued my tour, I saw the truth of what he had told me everywhere I went. I saw joy, peace, and harmony in the souls gathered in stores, cafés, and galleries. I saw lovers holding hands, parents and children playing, and siblings and friends learning together. I did not see any emotional or physical violence. There was also no dominance or abuse of power. My angels explained that it's easy to live love in heaven, but the love we live here is only practice. I learned that our time on Earth tests our eternal soul wisdom about how to behave with love even under the duress of physical fear and emotional suffering.

Along with the celebration and perfection, I saw an abundance of diversity. Each neighborhood had its own distinct flavor and architecture. Some places were like the best of New Orleans; others were perfect examples of rural Tuscany villages; others still a Bedouin desert encampment. What each neighborhood had in common was a delightful near- perfection of form and ambience. The buildings were at their most symmetrical, the food was beyond delicious, and every person did his or her job and got along with others with grace and humor. After taking in all this beauty, I had one of the most startling realizations I was ever to have in heaven, or on Earth, for that matter.

I kept seeing pieces of heaven that looked so earthbound, I would have sworn I was back on the planet. Usually places in heaven have an aura of love and radiance that creates a transparent look. Some of the places I saw were surprisingly solid, less transparent, even though they retained that same aura of light and love. I asked my angels what this difference was about, and they told me that heaven is a very separate reality while simultaneously being in and around each one of us on Earth at all times.

They told me there are places and moments in life that reach the perfection of the union between heaven and Earth. Those moments embody the foundation of all creation and all being. We are slowly, achingly evolving toward every moment of life being like these perfect moments. On my tour, I was seeing the potential of perfection for Earth that rests in heaven. Heaven holds the archetypes for all of this; the neighborhoods I was traveling through embodied them.

My angels took me next to some neighborhoods where people went to heal from cruelty and tragedy. I was glad to see that souls really do heal in heaven. I had spent a lot of my time on Earth worrying about the mess we humans seem to be in right now. I wanted to know what heaven was doing about that, especially what our loving Source was doing to stop cruelty and suffering. Souls who did terrible harm to someone when they were alive or who had been victims of destructive physical and emotional violence were welcomed here with open arms. They were given respite in their homes and work and given loving attention until they felt free of their suffering. Heaven always tries to help souls heal from the worst that life can bring on Earth.

I was encouraged to see that there are active, rigorous attempts to heal everyone in heaven who needs it. My soul was still smarting from surviving my father's emotional abuse. I was also still bruised in my core from the betrayals I'd suffered at the hand of those who'd tried to rob me blind in business dealings. I had an urgent interest to find out what would happen to those who'd harmed me and my loved ones. I didn't want suffering to continue. I didn't want to see anyone punished or hurt; I just wanted to see the perpetrators healed so they would stop hurting others. If I could witness this repair work in heaven, maybe I could learn how to teach this kind of progress on Earth.

What I saw was startling; it rearranged my buttons. I was taken to the dining hall of a lovely dormitory in a neighborhood that looked a lot like an upscale New Jersey suburb. Its campus was small, beautifully landscaped, and close to a downtown village where the souls being healed could shop, eat, and commune with other souls in that particular heavenly neighborhood.

The large dining hall had many round tables adorned with elegant floral arrangements. One wall of the room was made up entirely of French doors leading out onto a lawn. It seems beauty is a key ingredient in anyone's heavenly healing process, and they sure had it in abundance right here. This environment was used by souls who needed it most. They had in front of them the hardest job of all: admitting to themselves they had done irreparable harm to a fellow human being. I was introduced to a man who had volunteered to share his experience with anyone who wanted to learn more about the roots of human cruelty as part of his atonement for the damage he'd inflicted while alive.

He was dressed like any suburban guy on the weekend—a nice polo shirt, chinos, and deck shoes. He was a strong, intelligent man who'd clearly opened his heart in order to take in loads of wisdom since he'd crossed over. I'll never forget the agony on his face as he explained to me that the hardest healing for him had been watching the consequences of his hurtful actions continue on even after his death. Angels in heaven gave him regular, compassionate, but very honest reports of how his cruelty was still harming his neighbors and family members. He had to see and hear the details of how a man he'd cheated out of a large sum of money lost his business, his house, and then his wife. In his family he had to witness his oldest daughter struggle with substance abuse as she tried to heal from his sexual abuse when she was a teenager. He had to watch his grandson slide slowly into substance abuse too because his mother's pain had left her unable to care for him the way he needed. And he had to watch all this without the help of denial or alcohol, without blockages like hatred and pain. Here he was fully aware of his responsibility in causing this pain and saw he could have prevented it all by being more loving and kind.

His task in this atonement was to continue forgiving himself—yes, forgiving himself—for his actions. His task was also to help search for and coordinate any angels available to send his loved ones and neighbors any extra help, in the form of loans, therapy, new jobs, or kindness- that they might be at all open to in their suffering. He had to spend hours beaming on their souls, praying they'd open their hearts and minds to this help even though he knew they suffered from the same anger and denial that had kept him from receiving heavenly help. Worst of all, he had to do this with their pain reverberating through his soul every moment they suffered.

The hardest realization for this soul was seeing that he'd chosen to incarnate this time to help the people he'd harmed in other lifetimes. But his own pain, fear, and lack of self-love had driven him to sin again and again. Because he had failed in his atonement, he would now have to stay in heaven without the option of incarnating on Earth again until every last consequence he had set in motion on Earth was finished for generations to come.

It could take eons to erase that level of pain from the planet. Eons! I couldn't begin to imagine having the joy and beauty of living on Earth taken away. No breathing. No chocolate. No *sex*! No music or sun-washed evening lawns, no touching, holding, and talking to loved ones again. Not for lifetimes. I couldn't fathom the horror of that. Life is brutal and rough, but without the beauty of life on Earth, all the bliss and joy you know in heaven gets to feel pretty surreal, maybe even a little empty. Without being able to return to Earth to express and continually reflect love and glory back to God while in human form, all that wonder literally backs up in your soul, and it hurts! Imagine going a century without having a good bowel movement even though you eat well every day, and you'll start to understand the kind of pain I'm talking about.

As the tour continued, I saw that this healing technique was also used for any souls who had chosen to be born for only one lifetime. If they enacted destruction during their only incarnation, they, like the fellow I just saw, must feel the reverberation caused by their victims' pain—and that of their children and grandchildren on through the generations—until the consequences of their actions are cleansed from the earth. During this time, they must also put aside their own soul development in order to beam love and help onto the relations of their victims until they are all safe and secure again.

This was very comforting to me. Seeing the divinity and humanity of the man before me in this cozy neighborhood -- even under the burden of his sin -- I felt love and compassion for him. It didn't matter that he was so much like the people who had caused me and my family the worst harm. I wanted this man to heal. I wanted him to love and forgive himself, and I wanted him never again to be capable of harming himself or anyone else. I wanted this for him, because seeing the heavenly neighborhoods I passed through and the love I experienced within the embrace of my Creator had completely altered the way I now looked at everything. I was remembering that all the structures of society and daily life are in place to help us live love toward each other in daily, active behaviors of kindness.

To put it simply, we take mortal form to celebrate the miracle of loving one another because in order to love in the fullest way, we need eyes and voices and arms and hearts to do it with. And all of life on Earth is geared toward supporting our bodies in order to express this love most fully. But even as I felt compassion for this fellow-- and for all the souls who had strayed from love in their lives and their choices -- I started wondering about evil. I wondered if it existed on its own, as real an entity as all the love I was immersed in here in heaven. Even though my body was gone, the memory of feeling something I had at the time called evil was not. While alive I had believed there was evil in the world; now that I had seen so much about love on this celestial journey, I was eager to know more about the force I'd always thought of as the polar opposite of love.

One of my angels told me, "Saul, you need to be aware of the fact that every action you or anyone else takes goes into the fiber of the soul. Over a long period of time, then, all you do literally becomes who your eternal self is."

Another angel picked up the subject. "There are some people who do so many bad things over such a long period of time in one life, or in many, that the momentum of their destructive behavior takes on a force of its own. It creates a life force that becomes stronger than the loving intention in that person's soul. We here in heaven witness this. We see the person's soul caged in this destructive behavior, crying in agony to be set free. We see the person's rejection of any attempts at help and rehabilitation. These people become one with the force of evil."

"On a large scale, such as Hitler's attempts to wipe out the Jewish people, or on a small scale, such as with an unrepentant parent who keeps abusing a child despite the best therapy available, evil does exist. When it exists in individuals, it can congeal into group evil at any time, such as when the white settlers decimated the Native Americans in the pioneer days of the United States."

I took in what they were saying, and it rang true given all I had seen so far on my tour. It made sense that evil would not always be easy to name or read. They showed me one of the most insidious examples on Earth that's plaguing the planet right now, especially in America. It's found in many middle-class homes that, on the surface, look pretty and loving to society from the outside. Viewing it from here, I could clearly see how, underneath that veneer, on a soul level, there is a deliberate denial of the needs of the human hearts inside those pretty walls. In that toxic, artificial environment, no souls are being nourished.

It's as if this particular slice of society is focused solely on serving the needs of the flesh—plenty of toys, plenty of food, creature comforts, and good education—but there is no attention paid to the truest needs of the heart and soul. The elements of living that for centuries made up the spiritual rituals of indigenous peoples— things like grace, the mystery of life, living with respect for the self, and honoring the proper place of all life on the planet—have disappeared from childrearing. What a terrible negation of reality. From heaven, it looks as if a huge segment of people on Earth suddenly decided that no one would die from getting hit by a car, so they let their children play in traffic.

Because this level of active denial goes on all over the planet these days, heaven has decided any soul crossing over who's done extreme harm in his or her life will be surrounded by love and compassion—given a kind of etheric time-out, if you will—until the consequences of their actions no longer reverberate anywhere on Earth or in heaven. No matter how much these individuals might want to atone, to take on a task of service or to return to Earth to try again, they are required to stay held safely in living radiance until all the consequences of their destructive actions have been completely healed.

Needless to say, with some folks this could take forever. But that's exactly what needs to be done, because once the momentum of evil in your life has started, the road to recovery isn't easy. Heaven *can* help you transform at any moment, that is definitely true; but it's a long journey back.

Now, we all know that brutality, harsh realities, evil and random error permeate every day of our lives on Earth. They all make the love concept seem like a crazy joke by comparison. After all, it was the harshness of life that had caused so much misery in my life that I chose to die early just to get away from the pain. But now I was about to learn how love transcends these forces and how my soul purpose—the very defining, deepest desire we bring to Earth each time we incarnate—could still be accomplished even though I'd cut my latest lifetime short. My angels thought the best way to illustrate this was to show me four "chapters"—four of my many past lives from my eternal love story with Irene.

Now, you may or may not believe in past lives. What belief system you have is less important here than the basic truths I'm hoping our history will illustrate. Rather than trying to convince you of a certain way to look at things, I'm hoping you'll be willing to consider that there really is something eternal at work here. I don't want to define it for you. I just want to ask you to keep an open mind as you read, to remember times in your life when you had a knowing about the rightness of things going on around you, and how you trusted that knowing even if you couldn't explain why. Irene's a great example of a person with that sort of intense knowing. You'll see later on in this story the way she always knew and trusted that there was something more to our love—something larger, something intended to impact on others—than either of us could have comprehended while I was alive.

If you don't see eye to eye with the reality of these stories, then maybe you can just see it as a good love story. The events making up the fabric of Irene's and my love for each other hold an eternal truth that was so powerful, it motivated me to reach her across the divide between heaven and Earth. Whatever else you might get from reading about our passions, tragedies, and comedies, I hope most of all that you will see the bottom-line truth: the love you give and receive in your life now can and *does* go on. The love you manage to stumble through for your parents, your neighbors, your children, or your spouse, no matter how imperfect, *can* help stop the force of cruelty in the world and can help you overcome any tragedy life hands you.

I have to admit it took me a minute to grasp this concept of living more lifetimes than the one I'd just left. Once I did, though, the memories became more than mere fleeting thoughts. The first impressions of a lifetime Irene and I had shared a few centuries back came to me in a full-color, three-dimensional, movie-like panorama. My angels said they started me off with this memory to remind me why I'd decided to take on this last incarnation in America: my love for Irene and my desire to help others. So stay tuned for the beginning of our eternal love story as my angels led me through it, but first, here's how Irene learned about my death, was able to find and communicate with me, and identified our joint soul purpose.

Irene Survives the Crash

As they loaded me into the MASH-type helicopter that took me to the emergency trauma center after the accident, I felt how much easier it would be for me just to let go and die. But then I remembered the messages I'd gotten and knew I had to live. I connected with the medical team working on me, asking their names and even thanking them for their help. Their compassion was an additional inspiration to live the directive I'd just been given about being loving and kind to everyone.

That night in the emergency room, I appreciated every person who came near me as if there were rows of angels watching me, including the empathetic doctor whose job it was to give me the official news that Saul was gone. It makes sense to me now why heaven had asked me to be loving and kind to everyone: that way I consciously stayed open to all the love and support being sent to me through others.

The doctor who told me the news about Saul promised to be there with me when I had to tell the kids their father was gone. Dr. Jordan was a tailor-made gift from the angels. There I was, being treated in a Catholic hospital, yet heaven managed to bring me a surgeon to comfort me who also served as the assistant rabbi in his synagogue. I told the kids one by one. They poured their grief and sadness into calling friends, family, and business associates and attending to the details of the funeral arrangements. Sandi, Bruce, and Matt worked as a great team during those first horrific hours and days after losing

Saul. As I've always believed that family is so much more about love than blood ties, it was incredibly reassuring and rewarding to see my blended family cooperate so lovingly with one another. In the midst of this tragedy, I saw how all those hours in counseling and all those nights Saul and I had worried over and cared for these three kids now came back tenfold.

Three days later, I left the hospital to begin my new life without Saul.

About six weeks after the accident, I felt like I was living in hell. I'd participated in Saul's funeral. I'd survived shiva. I had begun negotiations over a ton of delicate family issues, and I was struggling to cope with the demands of a complicated real-estate development business. I cried myself to sleep at the end of every long, problem-filled day. Despite the love and help of friends and family, I still felt totally alone.

Then one day I got a condolence call that started me down a whole new path. It was from my dry cleaner, Joel. Several years ago, after tragically losing a son, he'd been counseled by his grief therapist to try contacting his son on the other side. He told me how positive his experience had been; it had helped him heal and go on. He recommended I see a medium named John Edward because of the unique, humorous, and very touching way he had of helping people commune with the souls of loved ones who'd crossed over.

I hadn't believed in any of this stuff before Saul died, but having received those incredible messages, I knew there was a bigger reason for my having survived the accident. Those messages had intensified a feeling I'd had since I was a kid that I had some specific destiny to fulfill. Experiencing those words before and during Saul's death had broken through my skepticism, so I decided what the hell? Why not give this Edward guy a shot? I was missing Saul with every fiber in my body. Anything was worth a try.

Two weeks later, I went with Joel and his wife to an event hosted by John Edward. There were about thirty-five people there. I sat amazed as this man reeled off incredibly personal details from the deceased to their loved ones in the room. Soon it was my turn.

"He says he sees you're driving his favorite car with 'Saul Z' on the license plate, and that you're wearing his skier charm under your blouse." I was astounded. How in God's name could this man, or anyone else for that matter, know what I was wearing under my blouse?

"He's telling me the accident took place in a different state from where you live," he went on. "He's telling me three hours passed between the accident and the time you were officially told he was dead."

This was when I really began to know it was Saul, and somehow, in some way, he was communicating with me from wherever he was. These details about the accident were private to me and Saul, specific pieces of information, and they were *true*.

"I'm getting a feeling of a heart attack and of hemorrhaging around the heart. Is that how he died?" John Edward asked. It was. Something had penetrated Saul's skull, causing a chain reaction of internal hemorrhaging in the chest cavity that led to the heart attack that was the medical cause of his death.

Joel busily wrote down the messages for me as I reacted with a mix of tears, surprise, and elation. The rush of this communion with Saul convinced me that all I'd ever been taught by my Jewish faith was true: we *do* go on. Our souls *are* eternal.

My experience with John Edward went from interesting to wild beyond belief when he captured the essence of my ribald, loving Saul.

"Was he a real character?" John asked. "Did he like to tell jokes with accents? And did he own a lot of hats?" The answers to all these questions was yes. "He's holding up a can of tomato juice. He says it's about a joke between the two of you."

It was. When my son Matt was small, Saul liked to joke that he was so skinny, if you filled him with tomato juice he'd look like a thermometer. Now *this* was my Saulie!

"He's holding up two fingers on one hand and one on the other," John continued. "Does this have a meaning for you?"

It sure did. Saul and I had raised three kids together, his two and my one. That simple image summed up what had been the core of our marriage: creating a loving home for our blended family.

"He's telling me he knows you had a premonition that he was going to die in the accident." This blew me away. I had told no one— no one, not even Saul—that I had been given this information prior to the accident. Of all the details and pieces I got that evening, this was the one that really knocked me out. I mean, someone might have the psychic ability to read a person's mind or make educated guesses about how human grief works, but that spiritual premonition had been my secret. No one on Earth knew anything about it. For the first time since the accident, I actually smiled.

I was still grieving, but after this experience, the desire to hear from Saul again gave me something more hopeful to think about, including lots of questions that started popping up inside me. What would happen to Saul's and my love now that I knew there is life after death? Were we soul mates? I'd always felt our love was bigger and stronger than most. Now I was coming to believe we must have loved and lost each other before.

I started devouring books on spirituality, looking for anything that might echo what I was experiencing or give me some answers. My session with John Edward opened me up some to new possibilities, but I'm a logical, structured person. I needed to be reassured with supporting information. I attended classes about communicating with the spirit world, and, through one of those teachers, I got another message that turned my world even further upside down.

This message told me, though I have no degree in literature and no history of being any kind of public personality, to write a book about Saul and me. This book, the message said, was to center around our love for each other—a love that had spanned centuries. It was also supposed to be about how living love as a behavior toward oneself and others, as Saul and I had worked so hard to do, is the key lesson we all need to learn while we're here on Earth.

I was at a total loss. I had no idea where to begin.

So why did I take this leap of faith and begin writing this book? To tell you the truth, it was because I'd found Saul again. When he had been alive, I had devoted my life to helping him. And through those "conversations" with him, I knew that Saul needed me to do something for him now. Whether it was because I still loved him so much or because I was still in the habit of doing things for him, I knew I could not turn my back on him. So I took the leap.

Not long into the writing, however, I realized I needed help. I needed more answers. Were we indeed soul mates? Had we lived many lifetimes together? Why did Saul have to leave me? How come I still had to do this work when he wasn't around anymore to help me? And where the hell could I go to get some answers?

As if in response, my phone rang. It was my sister-in-law Carolyn.

Carolyn is a spiritual healer and teacher. When Saul was alive, he and I had believed that what she did was ridiculous, but I'd had a change of heart when Carolyn told me that just after the accident, she had received some messages from Saul. Just the other day, she was telling me, she'd picked up one of her books on spirituality and a piece of paper had fallen out of it. It was an ad from a local metaphysical center that had on it the name of certified psychologist: Joan Pelham. One of her main services was spiritual grief counseling. I called her immediately for an appointment.

I was greeted at the center by a beautiful, blonde woman who turned out to be Joan Pelham herself. Even though I'd had success in contacting my husband through John Edward, I was still nervous about trying to reach Saulie again. It comforted me to learn that as a traditional psychologist, Joan had counseled families in hospitals, worked with children in public schools, and assisted police departments. She'd provided testimony and made mental-health evaluations for the Superior Court of New Jersey. It was during this period,

Joan explained, that she'd had an angelic experience and began receiving messages telepathically from the other side.

I was thrilled to learn Saul had communicated with Joan the night before. In fact she already had messages for me.

"The message above our bed says it all," he had told Joan. On the wall above our bed was a framed piece of pillow art of a man and woman walking down the aisle on their wedding day, very much in love. Another message was for me to go to our den, look at the third book from the left on the top shelf, and see what it was titled. The name of that book was *Israel, My Beloved*.

Next he had mentioned a scratch on the side of my kitchen sink, which he'd said needed to be repaired. I'd never noticed any scratch, but I looked closely when I got home, and there it was! Saul also told me to keep his side of our bed warm. There was no way Joan could have known I'd been sleeping on Saul's side of our bed. My dear husband really was communicating with me.

Joan received messages from the other side via automatic writing. I would ask her a question, and she would write down whatever came to her on a pad of paper in front of her. It was very strange to watch because when she was through writing, she would often have no recollection of what she'd just written.

Joan even received answers to questions about a business deal she couldn't have known anything about. There was also detailed information about people she'd never met. But my favorite message was this: "The most memorable moment of my life was when I looked into your eyes and said, 'I love you.' I remain forever in your heart and soul. We are merged as one. You are never alone, ever. Just trust that I guide you in every decision. No longer question what has occurred. Just know the last thing I thought of was you. I had no choice but to leave you. Now I will help you. Your hand I hold. My strength I give to you. I wait for you to glide gently into my open arms."

After I stopped crying, I reminisced with Joan about the incredible love I'd shared with Saul. When I told her how sensual our sex life had been, she smiled shyly and said, "I know. Saul just put a visual into my head, but I'm embarrassed to share it with you. It's very explicit."

With some prodding, Joan shared what she'd been shown. Saul had given her a graphically detailed description of our very last intimacy, savored in the hot tub at our ski house the night before he'd died. It was totally accurate. I left Joan that day excited and hungry for even more messages from Saul. I was missing him more than ever.

I was becoming convinced the connection between Saul and me had to be a lot deeper than one lifetime. But Joan was not able to get information about past lives, so I asked Carolyn if she could recommend anyone who did past-life work. She told me she had great respect for a woman named Leslie Lynne, from whom she'd once taken a class. That was endorsement enough for me: I called Leslie the very next morning.

She had a very calm, soothing way about her. When I asked about past lives and the existence of soul mates, I was glad to see that all her responses were based in common sense and solid family-counseling theories. Leslie was definitely no wavy-gravy spiritual medium. That more than anything gave me hope that maybe now I could get some real answers.

I asked her to tell me a little of her own history. She was a family therapist, she said, as well as a spiritual educator and went on to list some of the people who'd come to her for help. Former clients included rabbis, ministers, and doctors, psychologists, housewives, artists, and accountants. Earning a degree in family therapy, she said, had led her to spend twenty years counseling people in all stages of development and life struggles. What made her different from most of her peers, however, was that in her practice she also utilized her healing gifts.

Apparently, through these gifts, Leslie had been able to maintain direct communion with heaven for most of her life. Since the age of three, she'd been communicating regularly with heaven. By maintaining this daily level of faith and by constantly focusing on divine love, Leslie had developed a second sight that included being able to see people's souls while they were alive as well as seeing the impacts of their actions on future generations. Because of this unique blend of healing abilities, heaven had guided her to create a sanctuary where souls on Earth as well as in heaven could find resolution for how their actions affected the fabric of human existence. To facilitate her communication with all these souls in need, she had built a "healing cabin" on her land, which was sacred ceremonial ground for Native Americans in Massachusetts several hundred years ago.

She intently wanted me to understand that channeling, or *translating* as she called it, was not what she normally did in her healing sessions. She explained that although some of her sessions could include guidance or simple messages from loved ones who had gone before, her main focus was healing soul wounds, helping people to embrace their soul wisdom, and dealing with issues an individual suffered from during this lifetime.

Just as I began to feel excited and trusting about this down-to-earth person, she threw me a curve ball by telling me that, as we spoke, she was keenly aware of the essence of Saul's soul. If that weren't enough, she matter-of-factly stated that Saul needed me to help him.

When I asked her what he could possibly need me to do for him up in heaven, she said all she could tell me right then was that she sensed a deep, pressing need in him to work through issues that were left over from our marriage.

"Do you mean to tell me he's hanging around up there in heaven with God and whoever, and he's spending his time thinking about what we should've done while we were married?"

Leslie laughed, assuring me his concerns were based on the soul level and had more to do with parts of himself he'd shut off from because of the pain he'd suffered while he was alive. She added that one of the problems with being soul mates—and yes, she reiterated, as if she could hear my response, "You were and are soul mates"—is that sometimes the denial of one soul in the relationship can adversely affect the growth of the other. She said she wanted to get into more detail face to face. For the moment the only other message coming from Saul was that he and I had had a larger contribution—a joint soul purpose, she called it—that we would have made if the end of Saul's life hadn't been so hard and off-track. At that point, she said that I was free to do what I believed was right, but Saul's need felt very urgent. She recommended I come to her cabin as soon as possible, since my presence was apparently needed to complete this work, but ended by saying once again that I had to listen to my own wisdom and only come if I felt it would be the right thing to do.

I have to admit that a lot of this stuff sounded pretty far- fetched. I was trying to be open minded about this journey I had started on with John Edward, and I couldn't deny the comfort in Leslie's words. But she was a stranger living a simple life on a farm with her four kids. And there she was: sitting on that farm, having never laid eyes on me before, telling me Saul and I would be able to help each other heal and resolve issues between us from where he was. I weighed my skepticism against how genuine she really did sound. There was also the ringing endorsement my sister-in-law had given her. Looking back, I also have to admit there was a gut feeling urging me to go forward, but...I just didn't know.

Feeling vulnerable in my grief and wanting to let my skeptical nature lead the way, I knew I needed some reassurance. So I asked Leslie to let me think about it and call her back, and I immediately called Joan Pelham to ask her what *she* thought about this idea. She didn't know Leslie at all, but since I already trusted Joan, I told Saul through her that I would go to this healing cabin only if he truly believed it would help him. Joan lovingly encouraged me to go, telling me Saul had answered, "It will help both of us, so please go." I called Leslie back and arranged a time for the meeting that would change my life.

Three weeks later, I pulled into the dirt driveway of Leslie's farm in my brand-new, luxury-edition Audi Quattro. Stepping out in Italian shoes and my favorite velour coveralls, my hair and nails just done, I couldn't help feeling that I was walking into a third-world country. I was a complete foreigner standing near the shabby farmhouse and staring out at the sheep-dotted pasture on either side of me. I figured I should walk up to the small, simple wooden cabin that stood alone in yet another field, since that was where Leslie had told me we'd be having the session. But the door was closed, and I wasn't sure what to do, so I nervously paced back and forth on a small patch of mowed grass close to the driveway's edge. I knew I was perfectly safe there on the warm, late-fall day, but I kept looking over my shoulder any-way to make sure nothing was planning on springing out from behind some bush and attacking me. I just couldn't relax. I wanted to start. I wanted her to be the real thing, and the suspense was killing me.

Finally the cabin door opened, and there Leslie stood: a tall, dark-haired woman, simply dressed and barefoot. She said good-bye to the client just finishing a session, then she smiled and waved at me to come on in.

We introduced ourselves, and then she told me to sit down on a rough, hand woven rug spread out in the center of the dusty floor. I complimented her on the beautiful pattern of the rug as I tried to get comfortable, and she told me she'd woven it herself with hand-dyed wool from the sheep on this farm. What she liked best was that it held the accumulated prayers for help, healing, and mercy of everyone who'd ever come to her cabin.

She told me that one of her primary healing resources was the Medicine Way she had learned first from her Native American ances-tors and, later, on her own. What she loved most about these teach-ings, she explained, was that they provided her with an ancient, longstanding knowledge that our souls live on after death. This way also had great respect for the fact that we can communicate with each other through the divide between heaven and Earth.

Keeping with that tradition, then, she wanted me to sit in the position of the north. According to the Native American Medicine Wheel, this is the direction from which we all receive wisdom and balance for healing. She waited a moment, but all I did was blink dumbly at her. I didn't have a clue which way north was. She smiled at my expression and pointed to her right. I shifted myself around and was about to ask her another question when she bowed on her knees in humble devotion before a simple altar, her palms stretched out in front of her, forehead to the floor.

I wasn't sure what I was supposed to be doing, so I looked at another tapestry hanging on the wall to my left, breathing carefully in and out to try to relax. Suddenly, she sat up and, with eyes closed, began chanting loudly and with great enthusiasm. I'd never heard the songs she sang, but they were pretty, simple and full of devotion. Her movements and chanting reminded me of the praying rabbis at the Western Wall in Jerusalem.

When she'd finished, she moved toward me and carefully placed a hand on the top of my head. Throughout the session she would gently explain to me what she was sensing in my body and soul that needed tending to as she worked on it.

The first thing she saw, in my heart, was that there were some pieces of me that I needed to reclaim from Saul.

"Actually, I sense two things coming from your soul very strongly, Irene. The first is how incredibly deep your devotion to Saul runs in you. I can see about a half dozen lifetimes in which you were together and very much in love.

"The second thing is you have an immense, aching need to complete the work you came here to do this time around. It's interesting to me that—" And she cut herself off in mid-sentence.

"Are you all right?" I asked. I was lying on my back at that point, and her right hand rested on my solar plexus.

"Yes, yes, sorry. I'm fine." But she still looked distracted to me. "Where was I?"

"You were saying something about the work I wanted to do here this time," I said.

"Right. Thank you. We'll get into that in a minute. First there are some things I'd like to heal on the body level. I want to work on your right side, which is a real mess."

"Well," I started explaining, "that's the side of me that took all the blows in the car accident."

"Would you mind telling me a little more about that?"

"No, not at all." And I did, but for some reason it was hard to relive it all with her in that little cabin. It's hard to describe, but there's something about this kind of energy work that brings out or magnifies powerful memories or emotions. Needless to say, I started crying. It got so bad I had to sit up. She brought a tissue box closer to me and held my hand until the tears slowed.

"Don't worry," she whispered at one point. "I'm used to this."

She was able to do some more healing, but two more times she did that same thing where she stopped herself in mid-thought. Finally she sat back on her heels, put her hands on her hips, and looked straight at me.

"He's here, you know."

"Saul?"

"Oh yes. He's right over there." She pointed to the far corner of the cabin.

"How do you see him? I mean what—"

"He's kind of like a hologram, clear and diffuse, yet the image is filled with the radiance of his soul."

I had no idea what the hell she was talking about.

"He's wearing khaki pants, a cream-colored shirt with blue pin-stripes, and blue-green loafers that must have been his favorites because they look really worn."

I don't know how she knew it, but that was exactly what he had worn the last weekend we had been together.

"He's telling me how desperately he misses holding and touching you. He says he misses chocolate and worrying. He misses seeing and hugging his kids…"

All that sounded like Saul, but it could have been true of thousands of people. She went on.

"Now he's telling me that his memory of the sun on his skin and the breath in his lungs is enough to make him ache with unbelievable longing to be alive for even one more hour on Earth."

Leslie stopped and looked over at me. I think she was expecting me to be more skeptical, but the truth is my response to these messages was a lot like all the other times I'd tried contacting Saul since he had died. I waited for her to continue, but she just sat there.

"Leslie?" I asked.

"Okay," she said, though not to me. Then she looked at me, tilted her head a little to one side, and said, "I have to tell you something."

"Okay," I said, wondering what could possibly be going on now.

"I'm trying to think of the best way to explain this to you. Normally my practice is limited to healing people. In the process of these sessions, I do sometimes hear from a client's loved one who's now on the other side. I've found over the years that most souls who go through all the trouble to push through the ether and my brain to talk to someone here on Earth normally have a simple thought or concept they want to share. It's rare that they're interested in sitting around and having a full-out conversation. Also, when I say I hear them, what I mean is I take in the energy they are putting out at me and translate it into words that come as close as I can sense to what they might want to express. Am I making any sense?"

"Oh yes," I said. This was more information than I'd gotten from any of the others who'd channeled Saul for me. I was fascinated.

"And the *only* reason I'm willing to communicate with someone on the other side," she continued, deep in thought, "is to clean up patterns left undone from their death. Saul is here with us right now, and one of the things he needs to clean up is to apologize to you for withdrawing emotionally during the last few years of his life."

She was right about that—Saul had withdrawn further into himself. It was one of the things that had made me worry so much about how hard life had been getting for him at the end.

"He's saying that he…umm, he wants to…. Wait a minute…." She sat as if listening intently to something or someone. "I'm sorry, Irene. I don't know how else to say this except that your husband is one of the loudest, pushiest souls I've ever met!"

I laughed in full agreement.

"Normally I'm able to speak *for* the soul," Leslie went on, "translating, as I said, in order to get the gist of what they want to say. But Saul is so clear, and so...*loud*, Irene! He's all but screaming at me to let him come through and have a conversation with you. I don't believe in that, and I almost never do it. In order to be that sort of channeler, you have to push your entire personality out of the way and literally give your body over to another soul so they can use you to talk. It's very uncomfortable, and I don't think it's a good thing for me or the person on the other side to do. But he will not let me work on you in peace, Irene! I'm not kidding. He's telling me I should trust him, that he desperately needs to talk to you without the restriction of my interpreting. He's just adamant. I can't get over this!"

"Well, I'd love to talk to him, Leslie, but if you don't feel it's the right thing to do, then I don't want you to." I was lying, of course, but I knew it wouldn't be fair to get something for myself at her expense.

She looked at me directly before smiling and saying, "Now, you see, that's the reason right there that I might just have to trust him and let him come through. It's your integrity, Irene. You don't know how often, as a healer, I watch people come in here for help, but then they turn away from the things they have to do in order to get better. It's one of the hardest things about the work I do: I can help someone open more deeply to healing heaven love, I can awaken them to their soul purpose, and I can also get intuitive guidance about certain paths it might be best for someone to go down next. But the truth is, if that client is not willing to do whatever it takes to get better, to heal themselves of wounds either from this life or past ones, then all my caring, wisdom, and vision are for nothing. It's all wasted unless the client takes complete responsibility for his or her own life and healing process.

"Anything I or any psychic can give you by way of guidance is only potential. Everyone always has a choice. Not everyone I see chooses to take the help I'm offering. But there's something about you and this incredible energy I can feel in Saul's soul that makes me feel safe helping you two. You have a strength that goes so deep. I know you can handle the personal fallout that always happens whenever heaven comes through this forcefully. There's something very strong and true about the bond you two share. So I'm going to do as he asks. I'm going to relax and trust him. I'm going to let his personality access my brain and vocal cords so he can speak directly to you."

I couldn't believe my ears. This was almost too much.

"I do have one provision, though, that I'm going to say out loud so you know it too, Irene. I'll allow Saul to come through me, but I refuse to lose consciousness during the conversation. That's just too uncomfortable for me. So I'm going to let him in, Irene. It'll still be my voice that you hear, but he'll be using 'I' statements that refer to him, obviously, and you'll probably start to recognize the flavor of his personality as it comes through. Are you ready?"

I nodded cautiously. "Are you sure this won't be too unsettling for you?"

"No, no. Don't worry. In fact I'm happy to do it if it'll shut him up!" She laughed. Then she sat quietly for a moment, her eyes closed. She opened them and looked straight at me again. "You want proof that it's me, don't you, Irene?"

I didn't respond.

"First of all, I want you to know how glad I am to see you. I know Leslie started talking to you on the phone about our joint soul purpose, and I've got more to tell you about that, but when I got up here in heaven and found out I need you to help me finish my work, boy, was I sweating bullets!"

"Why?" I asked almost in spite of myself.

"Because I was terrified you wouldn't have the chutzpah to believe me and make yourself such a public figure by writing a book—and all those people who've been telling you you're going to write a book are right, by the way. That's one of the ways we're going to get our message out. But Christ, Irene, all I had to pin my hopes on about your doing the right thing was how much you trusted and loved me. I don't mean that the way it came out—that's a huge thing to rely on. But I'm up here, and you're down there, for Chrissakes! And you know how we didn't believe in all this life-after-death crap when I was alive. And now look at me: I've got to beg this woman for five minutes with you, and we can't even be alone! And look at her, Irene. She's nothing like the company we used to keep. We wouldn't have been caught dead taking a nut like this seriously back then. And get this one: normally Leslie wouldn't have anything to do with the likes of us, either! Well, let me tell you, heaven's having a good laugh on all three of us now because I need her, I need you to believe in her, and she needs to complete her soul purpose by helping us."

If this wasn't my Saulie, this soul sure had the same straight-talking approach to life my husband had had.

"Everyone up in heaven knew we'd be all right, though. They'd all seen the way you love me, and they knew that meant you knew me inside and out. With that kind of knowledge, they were convinced you'd be able to recognize my true essence anywhere and in any form." He paused. "Well? Do you recognize me?"

Part of me was so sure it was Saul, I found myself fighting back the desire to reach out and try to touch him. Of course if I could have, the first thing I would have done was kiss him. Right after that, though, I would've punched him right in the head for leaving me the way he had.

But I still wanted more proof, and I told him so.

"You got it, Irene. How would you feel if I told you everyone in heaven is rooting for you to get your soul purpose done because they all know what a pain in the ass you can be when you're frustrated by not having completed it? You know what heart palpitations you gave the caterer, the florist, and the musicians whenever you threw a party? Well, that's the same way you get up here in heaven when you're determined. If you don't finish your soul purpose before you cross over, when you arrive in that mood, everyone up here is going to run to hell to get away from you!"

This was getting harder and harder not to believe. Someone might be able to know something about Saul or our history, but to make a personal joke about me the same way he had when he was alive was really hitting close to home.

"Told you," he said confidently. "Now, listen up, Cuz, because I have a lot of stuff to tell you, and I don't know how long Leslie's good for."

There it was again. "Cuz" was Saul's nickname for me, and Leslie couldn't possibly have known that. I could feel myself getting more and more excited.

Poor Leslie. Saul talked nonstop for almost an hour about our joint soul purpose, about our past lives and how heaven works, the whole bit. He interspersed his monologue with enough details from our life together—like how we had first kissed and the meals I'd made that he'd loved the most—that I didn't need any more proof. I can't begin to express how rewarding it was to talk with my beloved Saul again and finally to get some of my questions answered. He explained that heaven wanted the book to be about our lives so people can have a model of living love as a behavior. In this way the Creator and our angels hoped the changes people might adopt from our story would carry on into their daily lives not only throughout this lifetime but on into generations to come.

The other piece of the puzzle he gave me was the picture of what our life together should have been if Saul hadn't needed to die. Originally we were supposed to have had a slow spiritual awakening and an awareness of our joint soul purpose—to remain this model of a healthy family that lived love as a daily behavior—much later in life. Because Saul had become too wounded in his soul to stay open to this, heaven had taken him early. Now, from the safety of heaven, as Saul's soul was healing, he had awakened to our purpose. Through my devotion to him, I was being led to an awakening of my own. To my genuine amazement, this information did not surprise me in the least. Somehow it all felt really right to me.

"But now that we're stuck with the situation as it is, Cuz," he said, "I need to talk seriously about *you*. Irene, you need to activate yourself, to get in touch with your own knowing. I can't stress this enough -- you have *got* to do your soul purpose now before you have to leave like I did. Because the truth is, once you cross over, you no longer have the tools you need to get your soul purpose done. You can't imagine the pain that causes in your soul."

"Well, Saul, you've talked about our joint soul purpose, but are you telling me there's something else I'm supposed to do on my own?"

"Yes and no. It's not like there are two separate things you have to do, but there are things in your life that need some attention. I know you're grieving now, but you aren't going to be feeling this bad forever, Irene, and when you feel stronger, you've got to take that desire to get the message out that love matters and goes on no matter what and open your heart to someone new."

"Are you saying it's my soul purpose to find another man?"

"No, Cuz, but it *is* going to happen. You are going to love again, and I for one can't wait to see you being loved and cared for. He may not be your soul mate, because I ain't giving that job up for anybody, but he will be kind and loving and all the things you need. You've got quite a few years to go before you're done this time around, Irene. I don't want you to be alone.

"But when I talk about what's personal to you, I mean you need to be a model for people on your own the same way our marriage was supposed to be—and was for some people. When you agreed to my having that emergency exit, you knew I'd find a way to find you from the other side, and you knew you'd need that contact in order to be reminded about love and how it strengthens you. That way you'd be able to finish the work you came here to do. And part of that work includes keeping the bridge between heaven and Earth alive in order to give people hope and faith to go on no matter what painful stuff they face. That's what you *do*, Irene. That's who you are to the core. Do you understand what I'm saying here?"

"I think so," I said. "I'm going to need to think about it some more, though."

"Well, of course you are. We've covered a lot of territory here today."

"I know. But while we're on the subject, I just want to know how people can know what their soul purpose is. I mean, I have you and Leslie here helping me out. How can others get that information?"

"Part of the reason healers like Leslie are working on the planet right now is so they can be resources for anyone looking for this kind of wisdom. But, of course, the answer is inside everyone. Let me use you as an example.

"Ask yourself: what has been the thing that you have been the most curious about your whole life, regardless of your anger, grief, or whatever?"

"I guess that I care about how people get along. I always want to know how each of us is supposed to survive the psychic and emotional pain of living. But how is that a soul purpose?"

"Hang on. The next thing you do is think about where in your life you feel the most empty. Ask yourself: what is your greatest dissatisfaction?"

"That's easy. Feeling ineffectual and invisible in the presence of others."

"Good. Now put those two together, Irene, and ask yourself what can you do about it? Instead of complaining, try to come up with a practical behavior you can do to make whatever it is you've thought of easier for you and for others. Use those two extremes in your life and think about them carefully. Keep breathing and being silent whenever you can, and the answer will come to you. It will. And when it does, it'll be so clear it'll seem obvious, like you can't understand why you didn't think of it a long time ago."

Our time was pretty much done for that session. Leslie was worn out, and she still had to get supper for her kids. But we were all three excited about what had happened. Over the next several months, Saul, through Leslie, would tell me about past lives we had shared as well as bring me astonishing information about the journey he'd taken since he'd left me that cold winter day. These sessions brought me great joy. They also helped me adjust to my new life alone.

Here's how it all began.

A Bowl of Olives

Yes, folks, believe it or not, Irene and I have been in love many times before, which has given us countless opportunities to witness the complexities of soul evolution. I've watched quite a few souls going through the trial-and-error process of reincarnation, and we are no exception, having annoyed and adored one another over and over again throughout time as partners and soul mates. When we first got together, we were two very different people living much different lives from the one we shared in New Jersey. In fact Irene was a boy named Ruvin. Here's how it went:

Because I've always believed in laws that help people get along in healthy, productive ways, I had chosen to manifest as a rabbi named Shimon. I'd always been very energetic and ambitious, so naturally I undertook to be the best rabbi I could possibly be, which meant I went a little overboard. I denied myself all comfort and devoted my life absolutely to study and prayer. Coming to the end of my life, I was like a dry old stick, and my soul was itching for a whole lot more in the way of human contact.

One morning I was sitting in the yeshiva—the school or gathering place where the Torah was taught—with students studying all around me. These were the days when the Jewish people still lived in their holy land, and yeshiva was held in the great outdoors. A little boy—Ruvin—walked up the hill to the olive grove where we all sat every day. He was very nervous about joining the group, but this child's intelligence was so strong that it shone right through his fear. Still, for two days he sat silently at the edge of the last row of students in my group.

On the morning of the third day, his desire to learn finally won out over his shyness, and Ruvin walked up to my side, brushed a dark curl out of his eyes, and introduced himself. Before I could respond, he asked me one of the most profound questions it is possible to ask.

"Rabbi, I'm curious. Could you please tell me, what does the teacher learn from the student?"

There was something in Ruvin's innocent wisdom and vitality that burst open my dry, tightly closed soul. I was filled with a gratitude that no love of the word of God had ever given me. It's hard to explain: I had been so shut away from simple human contact, and here was this child standing before me with such wisdom and simplicity. In that instant, he showed me the reality of why people are born at all. I saw that the love of God comes to its most complete fruition when human life honors heavenly wisdom. As thirsty as I was for a genuine human bond, I didn't realize the depth of that thirst until this boy's faith touched me like a cool drink of water.

I was literally choked up by this moment of truth and generosity. I coughed so hard, my yarmulke slipped off my head. All I could think of was how I could possibly thank Ruvin for this moment. The heat of the afternoon sun reminded me how essential water is for the survival of life, so I reached for the water gourd, dipped it into the bucket at my feet, and offered him this precious gift in return. It was the kind of moment when two souls meet and know they have found home in human companionship through one another.

Ruvin loved the Torah. He asked more questions, with greater persistence, than any student I'd ever encountered in that long, dry life of service as a rabbi. Through our communion in an honest search for wisdom, a wise, good bond grew and strengthened between our hearts. What I found myself learning from Ruvin was how much a human connection could illuminate all the great wisdom I was studying. I'd been so focused on excelling at the laws—the esoteric this, the Jehosephat that—I had almost missed the boat. For the first time, but most certainly not the last, Irene (as Ruvin this time around) would save my poor, driven ass.

Ruvin's pure, kind love for me as a teacher and the wise enthusiasm he brought to every text we pored over and argued about were the keys to unlocking my understanding about how heaven's love manifests itself on Earth. But I don't want to give the impression here that our relationship was all reverence and etherial radiance. We knew how to argue, believe me. We each gave as good as we got, and we both held firmly to compromise, all the while never sacrificing any of the truths about ourselves as individuals. To be absolutely honest, there were a few times we threw all rabbinical dignity to the wind and had a lovely, loud bonanza of a fight.

One evening over dinner, Ruvin got so mad at me for not seeing his point that he threw a bowl of olives at my head. Olives were like gold in those days; not only that, the bowl hit my brow and gave me a good shiner. Ruvin was horrified that he'd lost himself so completely, but would he concede his point? No way!

I have to admit now that he was right.

The sweetest memories of that lifetime for me are those meals I shared with Ruvin at the end of our long days of study. Most days he went home to his family. His mother needed care and attention, and there were still siblings at home who depended on him. But there were certain nights when he could stay late with me so we could spend time together reveling in conversation and prayer.

The ritual was always the same: we'd walk in silence together down the hill from the yeshiva gathering place. The quiet would help us clear our minds from the day's work. When we arrived at my hut, I would set out bowls of goat cheese, olives, and the simple bread that would make up our evening meal. First we would pray together. As we ate, one of us would inevitably bring up a personal opinion about God or our studies.

And this was where the real nourishment began for me. Our minds were unbelievably compatible. One minute we'd be discussing a specific point of the Torah, and the next thing we knew we'd be in the thick of a heated discussion.

Sadly this companionship didn't last as long as we both needed or wanted. Being so much older than Ruvin, I was the first to die. I did the usual crossover, arrived in heaven, and went through the requisite customized version of re-understanding.

I could see so clearly from the other side that Ruvin's company had been my highest human reward. Even though I was surrounded by all the celestial bliss heaven has to offer, I could not rid my soul of its deep aching for the friendship we'd shared.

All of a sudden, I *got it*: love is eternal. It *does* go on after our bodies are finished. I got that how I had acted and who I had bonded with while I was alive had eternally altered my immortal soul. I understood right then and there that this is true for all of us.

I also got that all the loving consciousness in heaven doesn't come close to matching the beauty of loving another human being. When that love is accomplished with integrity and kindness in the face of all life's fears and struggles, it becomes a common thread that binds together the fabric of human belonging and the planes of heaven and Earth.

Touching Earth

"**S**o where the hell is the love story?" I can hear you asking. Instead of a hot, romantic tale, this is all about two smart fellows who get together, discuss God, and throw olives at each other! Well, every love story has to begin somewhere, right? And the truth is, the best and most lasting loves are those that start and continue with friendship.

Passion, of course, is an entirely different matter. As far as I'm concerned, it's one of the best reasons to take shape in a body at all. But passion can be snuffed out in an instant by a violation of trust. A friendship based in love's passion and trust will grow over time and stand up to challenges better than an attachment based merely on lust. Irene and I would discover the joys of sex and becoming complete soul mates in our next lifetime.

Loyalty is another essential part of any good, loving relationship. And after that heavenly tour you just joined me on, seeing all those people being treated so mercifully, I couldn't stop thinking about how hard things were for Irene because of my death. I asked if there wasn't something I could do for her and my family right away.

My angels explained they didn't have the power to control or block the actions of people who had been cruel to me or who might be harmful to Irene in my absence. That was against the basic law of the free will each soul is given from birth. They went on to say that the most powerful tools available for help actually grow inside each of us. Without an open channel of faith, of knowing that love

47

and safety are always possible -- even in the riskiest moments -- the angels have no funnel through which to pour their love and power.

But there was something we could do for my family, they said. A group of angels came and sat with me, and together we focused love and compassion on Irene and our kids. We prayed for hours on end, focusing on my family and on anyone causing them pain in their personal or business lives. We perceived my family's thoughts about what would be most helpful for them in any given situation, and then we focused love on the souls of all involved.

For many months I watched as Irene would pray and then be comforted. I watched as she kept faith in my love even as the problems she faced seemed insurmountable. In those clear moments, I was able to see the light from our angels in heaven as it penetrated the souls of the people with whom Irene was struggling. I was able to see her mind and body filled with the light of my loving focus on her. I would see her confidence renew. I'd watch with pride as she found more effective ideas or greater courage—anything that would get around or through the pain and fear of those who, in their own blind suffering, were hurting her.

I watched it work. Irene began taking prayer out of the synagogue and out of the sanctuary of our home. She carried that faith into every moment of her life. Every time I quieted my soul and believed Irene could be helped by my love, I watched the light in her soul intensify, touching her heart and mind with courage.

The reason this happens is in any healthy human relationship, we weave actual soul bonds of love that can transmit heavenly light into the hearts of our loved ones. My care of and love for Irene all those years had woven such strong bonds from my soul core to her heart that I was now able to reach her with my love even from across the divide.

I watched her open to this help even when it didn't seem to be what she had requested. I watched her work hard to keep her faith through all kinds of fears. I watched her struggle to stay calm through situations that in the past would have put her right under the table.

Our eternal love enabled Irene to endure the pain of losing me without losing either her financial security or her newfound belief in herself right along with me.

But no matter how encouraged and relieved I was by Irene's progress, I knew she still lived on a planet where many people operate directly from their fear and pain. My growing concern brought back a memory of another lifetime we'd shared. There's no debating the fact that Italy, several centuries ago, was a hell of a lot kinder to Irene and me than New Jersey had been so far.

Light and Love in Italy

Yes, folks, the love Irene and I share has unfolded over a very long time. It is deeply interwoven with our soul development, to the point where we have shared and continue to share a common destiny. This is not necessarily true of all soul mates, but it was decided well before we incarnated as Irene and Saul Weinberg that we would share a joint soul purpose.

Before that time, however, we needed a lifetime simply to know each other more intimately. More biblically, if you will. That was Irene's idea, actually, when she crossed over after living her days out as Ruvin.

The wait for Ruvin to come back to heaven had been intolerable, but Ruvin wasted no time in reconnecting with me on the other side as soon as possible after he crossed over. He tracked me down and literally camped at my doorstep. At the sight of him, I was filled with the joy and delight of our relationship. Unsure what to say, I was cut off in mid-thought as Ruvin, straightforwardly, asked, "What form do you most want me in next time? I'm yours. You're mine. Where do we go from here?"

I had never been so flattered and terrified in all my lives. *Holy shit!* I thought. *Boy, have you got balls!* But I didn't hesitate for a second.

Understand that when two souls find the kind of harmony and love we'd discovered as Ruvin and Shimon in our yeshiva lifetime, an unbelievable urge arises once they meet again in heaven. The pull is all about wanting yet another chance to incarnate together in order to experience the tremendous joy of knowing each other sensually. It's one thing to perceive the truth and goodness of another soul up in heaven; it's a whole different, totally exquisite ride to add the touching and tasting and holding of each other's earthly bodies.

Having joyously agreed to be together, it was time to get down to the business of choosing the next lifetime and its million details. Because we loved each other so much, we planned a lifetime in which marriage would be our primary task. We vowed to be a shining example of what it means to give and receive love as husband and wife. We would be models of good economic and community membership, but we would also have plenty of time for great sex!

We manifested in Italy in the early 1500s, and our plan was to get together, have a brief courtship, follow the existing rules of that time period, marry, have a warm, loving marriage, and lead decent, caring lives.

We met when I was a little boy named Luigi, and Irene was a little girl called Maria. I remember looking over the bushes and watching Maria scrub her handkerchief in the stream. One time I even stole her pantaloons. There were countless times when I would do the silliest things just to get her to giggle. I have clear, warm memories of splashing and laughing with Maria on many long summer days when the hot sun danced on the water and our workload was light.

I grew to be a great clod of a man who was very proud of his physical strength. I was an ox for work, my magnificent farm producing more barley, grapes, and wheat than any of my neighbors. I really thought I was God's gift to the human race, I can tell you!

Maria, on the other hand, was very shy and very, very modest, which was certainly appropriate for that time and place. She would lower her eyes when I walked by, but even though that kept me from fully seeing her beautiful face, I always managed to spot the pulse that throbbed in her neck. I may not have been the most intelligent boy in the village, but I was certainly observant enough to find and cherish that sweet, subtle detail.

Before manifesting, we'd planned this little detail about the level of wisdom I would have (or appear to have, anyway) because we knew if a boy showed significant intelligence during that time in history, the family sent him straight into the priesthood. And we certainly didn't want that. I ended up not showing any sign of real intelligence other than the fact that I was attracted to Maria, so no one would push me into a life's path that would have led me to miss connecting with her.

I took great joy in my physical strength, my beauty, my humor, my sense of fun, and my devotion. I was a good son, a good brother, and a devout Catholic. My keen powers of observation helped me be a successful farmer. I observed the skies for weather and the bugs for information regarding any decay in the barley. I also observed Maria as she became a blossoming young woman. Whenever I caught sight of her drawing water from the well, I would become mesmerized by her innocence and beauty, her gentle care in the task at hand, and the pulsing of that vein in her throat (and how it got just the slightest bit faster whenever I went by!).

As observant as I was, I never once caught on to the fact that Maria was modestly and discreetly watching me. The fact that she was a bit younger than I was threw me off my game a bit. I had no idea of the power of her feelings for me, no idea of all she both feared and hoped for about us.

Maria was at once torn between her desire to make a beautiful home with me and her fear of a marriage to such a big, strong man. Over time, however, she noticed that even though I was large and ambitious and took up a lot of space, there was a deep gentleness in the set of my shoulders and in the way I used my hands. She also noticed the sweetness in my eyes and my smile. She began to awaken physically to me, to have an abiding desire to feel my tenderness next to her, my touch upon her skin.

Finally, after a long engagement and the whole nine yards—including my growing barley for her family as a bride price, and Maria sewing linens for a trousseau—we got married. We had a beautiful life together. We had a blast that lasted well into our old age. We often went to church and confessed we had allowed the sins of gluttony and passion to overcome us. This was not a lifetime that included children. We had made that tremendously wise decision before incarnating. We kept busy in this lifetime with loving each other, with art, with farming, and with community life. We had an innate disdain for any obligations that took our attention away from one another for too long a time.

Maria took great joy in living in our house. As a soul she had fallen in love with the fact that human beings had evolved to the point that they could build structures that passed from generation to generation. She also fell in love with the fact that people had evolved enough to be able to create beautiful things for everyday life such as pottery, carved wooden utensils, cooking implements, and looms for weaving fine sheets and cloth. We knew on some level that human beings were capable of using these tools to create daily lives that were less chaotic and violent and more centered in love and creation.

Maria had a love in her soul for order, serenity, cleanliness, and beauty, taking great delight in learning simple embroidery, spinning, weaving, and the ways of her mother's kitchen. We would sit together for hours, whenever the day would allow, and marvel at the beauty of the morning light that flooded our kitchen. That amazing light splashed the countryside at the top of the day and pulled itself across the sky in varying shades of gold and crimson as the day drew to a close. Our lives were perfect examples of the joy that can come from living simply and loving well. It was truly a blessed time.

Of course, all things must come to an end, and this lifetime was no exception. Later in life, I had an accident and was bedridden for a short time. I was not a good patient, but Maria managed to keep up with things and cope with my illness until I died. Afterward she missed me, but our life had been so deeply and lovingly lived she could feel me ingrained in her being even after I was gone. She was grateful I had suffered so little. Maria did not grieve for me as Irene grieves for me now. In Italy she was at peace. That is the gift of a timely death: it allows those left behind to grieve but not to feel ripped open by the loss.

During her last years, Maria lived happily with all the sweet memories of our life together. She enjoyed some peace and space in her daily life, in the kitchen and in taking care of others. Although she was courted by an older man in the village, she rebuffed his advances. During one very cold winter shortly after that decision, folks in Maria's community tried making sure she had enough to eat, but she was so old and tired she chose not to take as much food as she needed, leaving more for the children in the area. She died quietly in her bed.

The memory of Maria's death is so beautiful. As she lay in her bed, looking out the window, she saw me coming across the field with one of my scythes. It was a gorgeous spring day, and as Maria reached for me her soul lifted right out of her body. I took her in my arms, then carried her across the fields and home. When we arrived together in heaven, we knew that our hearts truly were as one, and we agreed that in the future we would forever be on Earth together as a married couple.

We learned from our lifetime in Italy that people needed daily access to education and some simple material comfort in order to help them improve their lives. Discomfort and brute hard work make it hard for most people to have an ongoing awareness of God in order to treat each other well and more lovingly. Small, precious changes such as these are examples of the way heaven attempts to continue bringing life on Earth closer to the joy of heaven.

We realized how, if religious education branched out into general education, then material conditions would improve at the same time, helping people have the time to contemplate and honor an ongoing awareness of God.

So, we began planning our next lifetime together. The problem was if we manifested again as Catholics at that time, given our level of deep devotion to God, we would've had to incarnate as a priest and a nun. We wanted to continue our relationship as husband and wife, so we chose to incarnate in a Judaic culture as a rabbi and his wife. It made me absolutely ecstatic that I could manifest as a person devoted to the Torah and have Irene by my side to adore, hold, and look upon. But Irene would agree to this only if she could be an intelligent, independent rabbi's wife at a time in history when women were being systematically shut out of many forms of social power.

Why not? I thought. We'd been blessed with unbelievable luck during these first two lifetimes. Irene and I decided to incarnate into a shtetl in Eastern Europe in the late eighteenth century.

Since choosing to deny the truth always produces or perpetuates human suffering, our angels knew it was important for us to understand the way denial destroys the fabric of human connection. We could understand this only through having this denial touch us personally in some way while in human form. Heaven was beginning to see how free will on Earth was being used to block the intention of the soul, which is always—*always*—to do good, and they needed our help.

It might have been a noble idea, but Irene and I were blinded by our optimism and good luck. We ignored the fact that Earth was heading for a time in history when friends and neighbors, blind with pain, became capable of ever-increasing atrocities because of the level of their denial. Instead we envisioned a plan that would involve expanding yeshiva education into the wider community and the joys such progress would bring. Rather than considering how such an event could come about, we deferred to the power of grace and mystery. The larger design of any plan always remained there anyway, so we confirmed our plans with innocence and inspiration.

How incredibly naive.

From Across the Yard

We were born into simple families, growing up as the proverbial boy and girl next door. I was named Yakov; Irene was Devorah. In this particular love story, however, the Romeo was not so outwardly strong and suave as the one Shakespeare gave the world. Lung problems since birth taxed my health and dictated for me a calm, solitary existence. As a result, I spent a fair amount of time in yeshiva, studying the Torah to prepare for my role as a rabbi. But since I was often unsupervised, I would move from my chair and sit in the doorway so I could watch Devorah, my young neighbor, play.

She, on the other hand, was blessed with vibrant health and an incredible set of lungs, which she used with great enthusiasm to yell, often and long, at the younger siblings for whom she grudgingly cared. I often saw her look with intense hunger at the yeshiva next door. Without ever talking with her about it, I was aware of her passion for learning and the fire of her anger at the injustice of her limited position in life. I could just tell.

My favorite memories of our childhood together begin after the day she finally got up the nerve to come over and ask me about what I'd been learning. She started coming every day, and, before I knew it, I was passing on my education to her almost word for word. She couldn't learn quickly enough.

It became obvious how much easier and faster it would be to teach her things if she knew how to read, so I slowly began writing letters and words in the dirt. It sounds like such a simple, harmless gesture, but back then I was not supposed to teach reading and writing to females. For many days, I carefully weighed my compassion for her frustration against my fear of being thrown out of yeshiva. Somehow my compassion and desire to be near her won. Before I knew it, she had learned enough to best me in almost any theological argument we had.

But, my God, the questions she asked! She had me coming and going, I tell you—just like she had as Ruvin in our yeshiva lifetime. Devorah even asked about the Torah's deeper meaning, questions that, because of their probing nature and their direct attack on the patriarchy, would have gotten her beaten had she had asked them in class.

Her frustration at this situation ate at Devorah like a cancer. One day, as she watched me deep in study across the yard, she said, "What do you have that I don't? The only difference is a penis! Because of that you get to sit all day and study Torah, while I'm kept here cleaning up after my family and rolling out noodles and wasting my mind on chicken dung and strudel dough."

I almost fell out of the doorway, I was so shocked. God forbid anyone but me should hear her say such things; it could easily have ruined her chances for marriage. That was when it occurred to me that she *would* get married someday, maybe even to someone else, and if she did, I would lose her. My feelings for Devorah started to get complex right about then.

It was around this time that she vowed she would someday create a role of greater power and independence than what she saw for the wives and mothers around her. She tried to spend even more time with me, pushing me to help improve her writing and share more advanced prayers with her. Devorah's capacity to learn was immense; the only thing bigger than her hunger to know was her desire to use that knowledge to understand her daily life. This was a leap I hadn't made, the connection between what I studied in yeshiva and what happened outside my front door. Her understanding of these complexities had shaken me to the core. Now my feelings for her were becoming even *more* complicated.

That's when the shouting matches began. I wanted to limit her education in order to protect her, but she refused to be limited. I was torn between protecting her and fulfilling her need to learn. She asked me to share with her the prayers in the Torah as well. Empowering her felt intensely important to me, so I took that risk. For her. I was growing to depend on the sweetness of our companionship. It genuinely illuminated my Torah studies. Her presence was like cool water during my dry days of studying and coughing in yeshiva.

This went on for some time, until one fateful day when we were sitting together in the dusty, noisy yard between our homes, talking and watching Devorah's brothers and sisters playing near the chickens. Suddenly she turned and looked at me. There was something very particular in that look, something about the way the sun shone on her curly dark hair, something that held my gaze on her in this full, silent moment between us. In that stillness, I noticed for the first time the way the life in her pulsed gently at her throat.

My God, I thought. *I love this girl.* All I could feel was an urgent love for her that pounded through me and settled right into the marrow of my bones. The deep wisdom in her little face awoke in me the knowledge that together we could be very strong, even powerful. As I looked deeply into her eyes, something sparked in them. That spark gave me the hope that she understood my longing.

Just when this moment threatened to overtake us both, her youngest brother, who'd been running excitedly all over the yard, tripped and fell on one of the chickens. While he screamed, the chicken squawked in indignation. Devorah jumped up, ran over, and pulled her brother up by the ear to get him off the chicken before he flattened the poor bird. Amid the squawks and tears, our moment was lost. She comforted her brother, and I went inside my house to pray.

And I continued praying every day after that. I prayed and prayed for the marriage broker to help me marry Devorah. I even went so far as to talk to my rabbi about my fear that she and I would be separated and unable to share God's wisdom together. Although my rabbi was not ready to believe we were divinely paired, he took mercy on me. He also figured it was in everybody's best interest to help this poor boy, addled with lust, from getting lost in his mooning and anxieties.

There was a marriage broker in the community who had known Devorah since she was a baby, a woman who had a very high opinion of Devorah's intelligence. The rabbi went to her, and the moment he mentioned I was interested in Devorah, she agreed it would be a good match. She and the rabbi approached our parents, and they all agreed to it as well.

I had to wait three long years for Devorah to be of marriageable age. I watched as she slowly stopped playing and began to help her mother in the house. I watched her grow aware of herself and become shy of me. She was pleased the marriage broker had picked me for her, not only because I was the only one who had fed her passion for learning but also because I made her laugh. She was also fiercely protective of me because of my many illnesses and wanted to live with me so she could take care of me.

During that time, we also prepared for one another. Since Devorah would be marrying a scholar and would need to help support the family, she had to learn a skill. Her father took her to market with him twice a week and taught her how to buy and sell vegetables from local farmers. He taught her how to deal well with Jewish folk and how to protect herself against unfair treatment from the Gentiles around us, many of whom hated our community and tried to take advantage whenever possible. I continued studying and praying my heart out.

In time my prayers were answered, and we were married. And the first surprise we experienced together was the deep joy and fun we got from lovemaking. In all their careful planning and preparations, no one had taken either of us aside to tell us about the mystery and heat we could inspire in one another. Outwardly, we focused on being a good, young Jewish couple—the community symbols of tradition and rectitude. Among others, we were careful to control our passions and remain dignified in the face of our new love. But once we closed the door on society, we went at each other with a fiery kind of madness.

I will never forget the silkiness of her skin. When my lips kissed the pulse at her throat, I knew no prayer could be as pure as the fire she inspired within me. She put all her fierce life force into pleasing me. She took me with such passion, often and gladly, that I was sure our neighbors would find me dead in her arms, having been racked with a fit of coughing at the height of our pleasure.

Our love continued to thrive over the years. We had two beautiful children. Despite miscarriages, poverty, and the perpetual fear of persecution, we were happy together, at least within the walls of our home. Outside them was a different story.

We watched as the Christian community frequently allowed Cossacks and farmers to steal from our merchants and harass our neighbors. We alternated daily between feeling pity for the poor, twisted souls of these persecutors of our village and a driving urge to do something to prevent further tragedy. We shared many long discussions about possible ways in which my teaching at the yeshiva could include the whole community so that everyone might become more protected from the risk of persecution. We felt if we could teach our neighbors about using the wisdom in the Torah to have greater faith in heaven's desire to help them, they might be less steeped in denial—the denial we all lived in over how at risk we actually were of falling victim to the Gentiles around us who frequently erupted into violence. Devorah and I understood this denial: if we and the people around us gave in to our gut terror at the permission the Christians felt to wipe us out at any moment, we wouldn't have been able to function at all. We would have just run screaming into the night like babbling idiots.

But a little release of denial wouldn't have been so bad. A little more soaking in faith and prayer together on this particular issue might have opened our poor, stubborn brains to some constructive ideas. Our concern was so great, we even dared to bring it to a few others of our faith whom we could trust with such radical thoughts.

Tragically, everyday life and the constant intrusions from outsiders made it impossible for us to create the very help needed to stop this cycle of rage and violence. One day, in drunken abandonment, some Gentiles from a neighboring community tore through our entire shtetl. Roaring and cursing through a gray, cold dusk, they lost control in their rage and inflicted greater and greater damage inside each house they entered. Every act of violation seemed to feed their hunger for more. Their gut humiliation at their own inhuman behavior goaded them finally to kill and rape.

You see, these men had been downtrodden by the rich their whole lives. Their dreams of freedom, dignity, or abundance for their wives and families had been thwarted countless times. That kind of lifelong disempowerment becomes unbearable to anybody after a while, and that agony often boils over into violence toward strangers. This violence gives the soul and heart a few moments of relief, a release found in the power of having someone's safety at your mercy if only briefly. But, oh, how the shame that follows being brutal -- even in small ways –either to loved ones or neighbors creates further agony in the soul. Eventually, this stew of disempowerment and cruelty to others boils over in a rage that seems uncontrollable and deepens with each destructive act.

I was at prayer in temple at the far end of the shtetl on the day these men erupted in pain. Devorah returned early from market, having seen the trouble brewing that afternoon. Simon and Rachal, our children, were in the care of our neighbor, Miriam. She had hidden them and herself in her root cellar, but Simon had slipped out, fearful that a prized copybook of his might get lost in the destruction.

Just as Devorah arrived on our lane, I felt an enormous wrenching pull, a physical lurch in my soul. I ran from temple, speeding through crowds of children, around men putting out fires, and past terrified adults fleeing everywhere in panic. Devorah arrived home just as Simon ran into our house. She screamed at him to come back, but it was too late. She could see the shadows of men moving inside our home, setting fire to the curtains with our own Sabbath candles.

Thinking only of Simon, Devorah ran forward and crossed the threshold in time to see the men smash his skull with a fire iron. She pleaded for his life, but her pain only goaded them further. They killed Simon with one last blow. The six of them then circled around her, raped her, and, when they were done, literally beat her into the floor with their fists, their feet, and broken-off table legs before delivering a fatal blow to her skull. They killed her with a cast iron skillet we had received from her parents on our wedding day. In the time it had taken me to struggle from temple to home, all had been lost.

The fire had choked itself to a low smolder, and Devorah's and Simon's murderers were gone by the time I got there. I don't believe I have ever felt any soul agony as powerful as that which ripped through me as I looked upon the two of them broken and shattered inside the shell of our home. I sat there in horror and shock, cradling Simon's small, broken head in my lap and rocking back and forth in prayer over my loved ones. I remembered Devorah's sweet pleasure and the power of my desire for her the night she and I had conceived Simon. He had come into being drawn by our sacred love. Within him, I had placed all my hopes for the future, and now they were both gone forever.

For the rest of that lifetime, that was it. I maintained my dignity, taking the best care I could with my work at the yeshiva and in the community, and I gave whatever love I could to Rachal, my darling girl who had survived the horror. But it was hard for me, especially as a rabbi, to make peace with the harsh dichotomy of trying to carve out a life filled with prayer and love amid the ever-increasing insanity and hatred of our larger society. It took me the long years of the rest of my life to get that balance right. I finally did come to earthly peace and grow an ability to embrace God's love and our human capacity for atrocity, but I was bone tired by the time I reached that peace.

My God, was I tired right down to my corpuscles. The strain of staying open to God in prayer and not getting lost in hate or despair while remembering every day the atrocities that had taken my family were enough to put a lesser man right under the table. By the time my appointed hour was close, I was even too tired in my soul to let go and die, for God's sake.

So once again Irene, as Devorah, came and hauled me out of my misery. I had been ill in bed for a few months. Rachal, God bless her, had set me up in her front room and had the patience to keep me clean and feed me soup even though I dribbled in my beard on a regular basis. Devorah took pity on me and, being so intelligent and knowing me so well, understood that humor would be the best way to get me out of there.

One day I looked up, and, by God, there she stood at the end of my bed in the form I most liked to remember her. She was wearing a dress she had worn often in our young married days, right after she had had Simon, her favorite gray shawl, and she had a huge grin across her face. Devorah, being Devorah, had no patience for my rabbinical dignity and my aged sorrow. She laughed at me. Laughed!

"Look at the shape you've gotten yourself into, Yakov," she teased me. "You've come a long way since the day you fell in love with me in our dusty yard. I don't know if I'd fall in love with you the way you look now."

"Devorah!" I cried. "Have pity on me. I've been through hell since I lost you."

"Oh get over yourself, Yakov. You've seen worse, I'm sure. Come on, lighten up a little. Do I need to bring that chicken in here and have my brother fall on it again?"

That made me laugh. Her brother had looked so utterly ridiculous sprawled on that chicken, and she had been so furious he had interrupted our romantic moment. When I laughed, I suddenly remembered how good it felt all over to be loved by Devorah. That did it.

My soul loosened up, and I smiled at her with all my heart. She tugged on my beard and laughed with me.

"Come on, you *putz*," she said to me. "There are some of the wisest rabbis in the history of time waiting for you right now in heaven."

That got me up and out. I left my body and hugged Devorah with all my might. Man, she felt good after all those years. Our souls merged and the beauty of her love gave me the courage to surrender to the void. We crossed over together. Waiting to greet me was my Simon. I held his soul with my own and cried with joy to see him again. It brought me such comfort to see him whole and unbroken.

And then I saw the souls of the men who had massacred my wife and child. They looked fevered with agony over what they had done; and they had been waiting quite a long time to beg me for forgiveness, because once a soul has done such a horrible act, their fate is really in the hands of those they harmed. These poor, beggared souls knew that until I forgave them, they would not be able to complete their soul development.

Devorah said to me, "Yakov, I have forgiven them. Now it is up to you."

I looked at them and said, "I spit on you!" There was no room in my heart to forgive them at that moment. I would later do a lot of work on that particular wound, which would enable me eventually to forgive them, but it was one of the hardest things I've ever had to do. To be truthful, I do not feel this was right even to this day. On one level, with all my compassion, I did forgive them; on another, however, I feel what they did was so far beyond any human cruelty I had ever witnessed that I actually questioned the justness of forgiving these men. It seemed to me to mock the very meaning of the word *forgiveness*, making the act itself further permission for them to go out and harm again.

Finding Worth

When you remember pain with your bare soul and without the benefit of denial, your soul trembles. It keens and vibrates with the searing knowledge of how the cruelty you have caused or received will affect you and many others for generations to come.

In that moment of facing those poor souls, a part of me understood how I might have committed the same atrocities if I'd been suffering their same level of pain. With that new understanding, I began to see precisely the way denial worked. Looking at them, I could see the way their pain literally created blockages in the light of their souls, which, in turn, inhibited their ability to stop themselves from doing harm while they were alive. It blew me away to see how thoroughly the denial of their own pain and harmful actions on Earth carried over into heaven. It all had not died with their human lives.

Alive, these murdering individuals had been unable to allow their souls to keep their hearts, minds, and hands from violence, which left them capable of unimaginable destruction. The shame over how they had behaved created a gap between their personal emotions and their eternal souls. This was what made up the blockages I could see in them; this was what prevented them from receiving mercy and self-forgiveness in that lifetime, in heaven, and in many lifetimes to come.

At least the cruelty of these men didn't stop Irene and me from living and loving again. I would've preferred to do without the cruelty in the first place—who wouldn't have? But there's no undoing what's already been done.

We also learned the hard way how difficult it can be to *find* your soul mate in a sometimes random, often crowded world. I tell you, there are few things more painful than confidently giving the target of your affection your biggest, most loving grin, your best opening line, and watching them look back at you in all their earthbound blindness and say, "Huh?"

The incredible connection found between soul mates is not limited to lovers. That's part of the interconnectedness among every person on Earth. Irene and I found there are also work and family soul mates. The influence these people have on your life, for good or ill, is just as profound as that of a love soul mate. The goal is always for everyone to help each other accomplish their souls' purpose, but all these relationships are at equal risk of being harmed by life's fear and pain.

I don't want to forget to tell you there are also important things to be learned when you're out on your own. At least that's what Irene finally convinced me of when she decided to incarnate alone. I still believe that what put this idea into her head was a very popular saying in heaven, which goes: "Fix yourself first. Find any place in your soul where you are part of the problem before you attempt to solve a situation." When she did this, Irene—fresh out of her Devorah lifetime, mind you—decided she needed a life independent of me in order to grow a stronger belief in her own wisdom. Plus, she said, I needed to practice letting her go. I had grown too attached to her no-nonsense guidance and her take-charge dependability.

She had a point there. I'd depended too many times on my social role to buffer me from the mess of human emotion. Let's face it: I was a wimp. I'd fallen into a pattern of thinking that said, "If I just kept manifesting and radiating loving wisdom no matter what folks on Earth do to me, everyone will eventually heal." What a cop-out. It was time to stop believing martyrdom was going to save the planet.

I'm making all this sound proper, organized, and calmly discussed, but nothing could be further from the truth. When she came to me with this plan, the *argument* went something like this:

"I'm willing to give you," she began in a ready-for-battle tone, "a lifetime in America in which you can give up your saintly attitude and instead become an example of integrity within the world of money and power. But I need the following: I need to live in a culture where I can help women break free of the chains of emotional and social repression. It almost killed me when those pogroms gathered, and I didn't have the money, position, or authority to protect myself or my family. I don't ever want to be that disempowered again. No one will ever take the life of a child in front of me again."

She paused for a moment, but I knew her well enough to know it was only for effect. She had no intention of yielding the floor until her point was completely made. Even the Creator knew it would be easier for everyone if we all just waited until she finished. She continued.

"I want to go back into the Jewish community. I want to be a single, powerful, brilliant woman. I want to receive a scholarship to a university and become a woman who earns her own living and uses that living to improve lives in her community. By doing this, I will heal my own wounds and be a role model of empowerment for many other women.

"If I do this first, then, when I live with you in America, I'll be a full partner to you. I won't lose my own voice to our social position or whatever else comes our way. I'll be able to earn money and have a political voice if I need to. I have to go back to the shtetl or to something else like it so I can—"

I couldn't stand it. I cried out, "No way, no how! Never am I going to let you go down to Earth to be vulnerable to persecution and violent death." Despite the fact that my heart was in the right place, it was definitely the wrong thing to say, and Irene let me know it, with both barrels.

"*Let*! What do you mean you're not going to *let* me go? Who gave you the right to choose for me? Back off. I watched you with your penis in the shtetl. Your male equipment was fabulous for giving me great happiness during many a night, but that damned organ also gave you freedom of choice, which I never had. And freedom from back-breaking housework, the pleasure (ha!) of giving birth, and the joy of being surrounded by children during every waking moment. Because you were a man, you got the beauty of studying at the yeshiva and learning to be a rabbi. You got the benefit of having a respected and honored social position."

She calmed herself down a little as she spoke. Maybe it was because she was wearing herself out. Or maybe it was the growing number of angels and souls nearby who seemed to be in silent agreement with the points she was making. She headed toward her conclusion even though she'd already convinced me with the word "*let.*"

"Now, understand: I loved being a woman. Making love with you as a woman is an experience I want to have many times over. I also loved the sheer power of giving birth and creating life as well as the power of my emotions and my intuition, and the way I used these skills to hold my family and our community together. But I *refuse* to have those gifts at the price of my independence and my ability to make my own choices. You want to choose for me because I feel all your feelings for you. You think if I'm safe, you're safe. Well, think again, pal!"

She was right of course, but I had to come up with the right way to lose the argument without looking like a schmuck in front of the heavenly crowd that had gathered. I said, "You know I only want what's best for you, but that doesn't mean I don't hate it when you're so damn smart, because I do. You're absolutely right—we'll do it your way. Only please, please let's set up a plan that has the most safety possible for you. Will you at least do that for me?"

That kind of request she couldn't refuse, so we sat down with the Creator and all our angels, and we planned a life for Irene based in an area of Eastern Europe that was somewhat tolerant of the Jewish population and was politically and economically stable at that time.

It was in a large city with a good university, and the timeframe of the mid-twentieth century left room for the social acceptance of educating women. But the timing, in order for me to reach adulthood after the middle of the twentieth century in America, would mean Irene would be incarnating in the middle of the upcoming war heaven was almost certain would break out. Terrified of this, I tried again to reason with her.

"You've seen what the Creator is fearing will happen to Jews in that war. How can you say this? *Do* this? Soul growth, schmoul growth! I don't care about that. I only care about you being safe and accomplishing your purpose. The conflicts in this war are going to be searing, inhuman, and heartbreaking. I don't want to risk your returning from a lifetime with a soul wound so profound that you're practically unreachable. Remember the souls we've been watching cross over lately? Do you want to end up in that kind of pain?"

Then Irene quietly, lovingly, reminded me of something I already knew but had, in this emotional moment, forgotten. "It will mark my soul more deeply if I hold my gifts back at a time when they are desperately needed."

I sobbed like a baby. My soul shuddered. I knew I had to let her follow her own destiny. We compromised on making sure her life would be purposefully brief so she could still join me in America as scheduled. That argument taught me never to mess with Irene's knowing again. She's got some killer instincts, that's for sure. And she was confident that, if given the chance, she could take a haven of learning and culture in Eastern Europe—as a Jew—in the 1930s and create for herself a badly needed sanctuary that would prepare her for her life with me in America. It made sense to her at the time that a model of equality in marriage amid safety and abundance should be built on what she would learn and what she could offer in a life I watched her, from a safe distance, get born into.

Sometimes I really hate being right.

A Soul Mate Alone

Born in Poland early in the twentieth century, Irene, as Riva, was an only child raised in a cultured, educated, and financially stable Jewish home. A bright, fierce, driven, and sensitive child with large brown eyes and a mop of unruly dark curls, she was blessed with a mother and father who lavished all kinds of care and attention on her. They signed her up early for music lessons, making sure she had all the help she needed to excel with the violin as well as in school.

Riva adored her parents. They were gentle, sweet, and kind. This lifetime, up until she was fourteen, healed her in many ways from the scars her soul had sustained through her death in the shtetl. She grew a quiet pride in her own intelligence, and she nurtured hope that she would somehow be able to use her gifts to be of real help to her community. She had chosen to be born with an open soul, you see, in order to be a conduit of God's love for the planet during this especially dark time on Earth.

It began for Riva with the disappearance of her violin teacher, Herr Schoenbrun. He had left on a music tour and never returned. As hard as it was to imagine all the things that could have happened to him, it was actually more painful for Riva to watch the way her parents pretended there was nothing abnormal about how a well-loved man with strong roots in his community could simply disappear.

Then came the government-sanctioned attacks on the store owners in her neighborhood. She began feeling more and more isolated as she watched her parents find yet another way to deny what was going on around them, another way to accept all the madness as a new way of life. They denied the import of everything that was happening: the new laws governing Jews' freedom of movement, the abduction of fathers and sons in the night, the uprooting and relocating of entire neighborhoods into crowded ghettos, all of it.

Because of her parents' refusal to see, Riva became the watchful adult. The last straw for her was when their rabbi was shot down in the open street after services at temple simply for not removing his *tallis* and yarmulke before entering a public place.

Riva's open soul and her common sense would not allow her to join her parents in their denial. She felt she had to do something to make a stand. Enraged, panicked, and desperate, Riva went to a neighbor and obtained false papers for her parents. She decided to send them out to her cousin's home in the country, where she was convinced that, if worse came to worst, they would be able to survive living off the woodlands. Riva chose to remain. Since she was sixteen at the time and very close with another relative who agreed to look after her, her parents accepted the plan.

On the day she took them to their train, she returned to the ghetto to find utter desolation. Soldiers had come during that brief time and rounded up the people who'd made up her neighborhood. They were among the first group to be taken to the camps. Anyone who had resisted had been shot. Bodies lay in doorways, in the streets, and in the halls of the apartments she frantically searched for survivors.

Riva finally found a little fair-haired boy, Fievel, quietly sobbing in a basement storeroom where he had managed to find safety. She gently led him out into the yard behind her building and into a garden shed. Fievel was one of Riva's favorite neighborhood children. He'd often sat outside her apartment on the front steps, listening as she practiced her violin.

Fievel's parents had helped Riva obtain the false papers for her parents. The soldiers who had come that day knew his father was involved in this kind of work. They had slaughtered Fievel's entire family: his mother, father, and five sisters. Fievel had heard their screams from the backyard, where he had first hidden when the attack began. Riva had seen his family in her frantic search for survivors, and she could tell by the look on his face that he knew they were gone.

Riva sat with Fievel in the garden shed until he stopped shaking, holding him gently while he fell asleep. She left him and went upstairs to his apartment, where she found him some clothes. She took his mother's wedding ring for him in case the world ever righted itself and he ended up with a future. She also took his father's tallis.

After she'd gathered up what she could, she knelt by the sides of his slain family members, folded their hands on their breasts, and said the prayers for the dead. Before leaving, she whispered to them, "May your souls know peace. I have Fievel. You live on in his courage."

When Riva got back to Fievel, she found he had awoken and, seeing her gone, had begun to sob again in terror. She did her best to calm him. After he was quiet, she brought out his father's tallis and his mother's ring. To comfort Fievel, Riva told him how she had watched his father pray in temple many times, how she'd watched his mother make noodles for Sabbath dinner and pray over the candles. She told him his parents were brave and good, and he must always remember them.

Fievel looked at her and swallowed hard before saying, "I would like to make my papa's tallis a flag to carry with me when we run away. We are going to run away from this bad place, aren't we, Riva?"

Riva got very quiet. It broke her heart to hear his desperate plea for escape. She could hardly bear the thought of using the tallis as a flag. To use it that way symbolized the fact that her world had been destroyed. But at that point, Fievel's well-being became her greatest concern. She knew he would need tremendous courage to survive, and she couldn't deny him this one simple request.

They would make a flag, she told him, to remind them of the love Fievel's family was sending them from heaven. But she warned Fievel that the flag was a secret that could come out only at night because they needed to reach safety and reach it quickly.

Something inside Riva told her the soldiers would be returning the next day to clean away the dead, take possession of whatever spoils they wanted, and kill any survivors they had missed. In the middle of the night, she bundled Fievel into a wheelbarrow along with their meager supplies and headed toward the country.

They walked, in all, for seven months. Wisely keeping to themselves, not even mixing with other refugees, they slept in barns and begged for or scavenged for food where they could. Riva poured every ounce of her energy into making eight-year-old Fievel as comfortable as possible. She had managed as best she could all that time, but winter was approaching quickly, and she knew they would not stand a chance of surviving if they didn't make it to a border and to safety by then.

Riva had heard some of the other refugees speak of a priest who was willing to trade jewelry or other valuables for simple clothing and food. She took the last pieces of her mother's fine jewelry to him to get some clothes for Fievel, a map of the area they were nearing, and a month's supply of hard bread and moldy cheese to help them through. Then she and Fievel set out on the road for the border Poland shared with Russia.

One afternoon they got on a local train to rest their legs and take a rare ride through the next few towns that lay closer to the border. Despite her bone-weary exhaustion, Riva had enough wits about her to keep track of which train stops were most likely to have searches. It was of the utmost importance that she remain aware enough to get off the train before they passed even one of these towns.

Unfortunately, two soldiers entered the train a stop earlier than she'd anticipated. When she saw them, she froze in terror, trying her best to act normally as the soldiers focused their attention on them. Fievel began whimpering in fear. Without thinking -- perhaps for the first time in months -- Riva slipped up and spoke to Fievel in French, which was the language she had shared with her mother during her most troubled times as a young girl. This immediately marked her as a cultured, educated person and not the Polish peasant she'd been attempting to pass herself off as. The soldiers demanded to see papers she did not possess.

When she was unable to comply, they grabbed the fair-haired Fievel from her and took him, screaming, from the train; they assumed the fair haired boy was Aryan. Riva would find out later in heaven that Fievel had been sent to the family of a local Nazi sympathizer who put him to work on a farm in exchange for sparing his life. Riva, however, dark-eyed and dark-haired, was pulled from the train and told she would be useful to the cause as a translator for the German army. She knew that translating was not all they would ask of her.

She spat at these soldiers offering her life in exchange for the one thing she would rather die than do. She called them pigs and inhuman traitors to humanity, swearing fiercely that they would never get her to serve them. The soldiers looked at one another for a moment. In silent agreement they dragged her through the snow to a remote corner of the woods. Riva did not make this an easy decision for them: she bit their hands, kicked, and screamed at the top of her lungs.

They hit her, punching her in the face again and again in an effort to silence her, but still she would not yield. As they tore at her clothes and forced her down onto the snow, as they held her down and raped her, Riva shouted Jewish prayers at them. She claimed a victory of her soul over theirs and continued praising the love of God over hate right up until the instant they emptied their pistols into her.

Riva lay dying in the snow for some hours after the soldiers left her. The despair in her soul had sapped her strength completely, and she was too tired and wounded even to let go of her own life force and make her crossing. Her angels in heaven saw her suffering and were searching frantically for a way to help her find release and come home. They finally hit on the idea of asking Herr Schoenbrun to bring her over with the music in his soul.

He trembled at even considering opening his soul to communion with Riva as she lay dying. His death at the beginning of the Holocaust had been brutal. He had reached some sense of peace and safety within his own being only after a great deal of healing in heaven. To open to Riva in love and compassion now would remind him of his aching pain, but there was no way he could abandon her.

He opened his soul to hers and allowed the pain in her soul to commune with his memory of a favorite Mozart concerto that held all the beauty of spring within its notes. Lying there in the snow, frozen and in searing pain, Riva suddenly remembered this concerto. As the memory of the notes moved through her, its joy and comfort opened her heart.

The music helped Riva let go. She arrived in heaven along with many others, all of whom were bruised nearly beyond their capacity to heal. The same wave of cruelty and denial we'd initially seen in our shtetl lifetime was now reaching a crescendo on Earth.

Choosing Birth

It isn't just the boundaries of battlefields that make an event like World War II have a global impact. Such a scourge affects us all because people truly are that connected. We are one, connected to one another through our soul cords -- like the way I stayed connected to Irene just after I died. This connection continues between all people on Earth; it is the fabric of human existence and is strengthened by our permanent union with God. Let me give you an example of what I mean.

At the time Riva lay dying in the snow, I was only three years old and living in America, but her death almost killed me too because some part of me knew that my soul mate was suffering unbearable agony. My mother reminded me of this when I arrived in heaven—how on the very day Riva died, I suffered a severe allergy attack. It came on during my nap and was so vicious I could barely breathe. My eyes swelled shut, and my swollen throat left me wheezing so hard my mother thought I was going to choke.

As those were the days before antihistamines were commonly used, there really wasn't much Belle could do for me except pray. "Please, God," she said, "please help my son. Don't let him stop breathing. Whatever he needs to help him live through this, please help me to give it to him."

What happened next is an exquisite example of the way heaven often answers prayers. Frequently it has to do with a greater picture that we in human form cannot even begin to comprehend, but believe me, it is help nonetheless. In this case, heaven answered Belle's prayer by helping Riva die and cross over in greater peace. Our angels knew that the agony of her death was causing my soul such distress, my immune system was being compromised. This is how deep my soul-mate connection is to Irene. We are inextricably linked: her agony as well as her joy are mine.

Within half an hour of my mother's prayer, my body righted itself, and I calmed down. Belle continued watching me carefully, but I never had as severe an attack again because Riva was safe in heaven, preparing to be born into a stable life in America.

Safely back in heaven, Riva/Irene began to heal. Although I wasn't there to share in her process, she could feel the intense pull of our desire to be together. The strong, unstoppable nature of our love for one another enabled her to remember both her larger soul identity and all the plans we'd made for our next lifetime together. She wanted more than anything, the chance to experience a lifetime in which we finally *accomplished* some manifest good. She needed a victory in a big way. All that coming and going, trying and failing, got pretty old after a while.

Despite the pull to join me in yet another lifetime, Riva/Irene was furious about what had happened to her this last time around. Understand that from this heavenly place of knowing, Irene could see the way the horrors she had just lived through would continue reverberating in some way for generations to come on the planet. As much as she wanted to be with me again, she was not convinced that the kind of life she longed for would be possible in a world still reeling from this level of cruelty.

The biggest glitch in Irene's efforts to get what she wanted was that our new lives were already in motion. If she wasn't able to heal enough to join me in America, I would have to live this lifetime without my partner and soul mate. Unwilling to leave me on Earth alone, Irene agreed to be born again and follow our plan.

In planning her life to come, she followed the path most souls take before they're born. Irene communed with her angels and the

Creator. She became silent to the depth of her soul and pulsed in rhythm with our loving Source. She quieted her ambition and enthusiasm and tried to allow the song of her soul to sing. She felt the joy and ecstasy of the song of life to her core. She aligned the pulse of her soul not only with the heart of our Source but also with the truth of her own being. It took all of Irene's self-love and compassion for her to choose a life that would be most in harmony with her soul purpose.

As these choices became clear, Irene's entire being pulsed in the rhythm needed to draw to herself the body, family, culture, and personal gifts through which she would manifest. She surrendered her whole soul to the heartbeat of life. A searing shaft of light imprinted her conscious being into the DNA and RNA of her future self waiting in her mother's womb. This melding of spirit and matter, this precious, utterly unique alchemy, was the beginning of my dear heart Irene.

Our joint soul purpose was to create financial and social security for ourselves while being loving to each other and our children. We encoded ourselves with the strength and compassion necessary to negotiate fairly even through the toughest issues that arise in families. We committed ourselves to loving our children with unending patience and caring, and we committed ourselves to living in cultural harmony with our neighbors and co-workers under even the most difficult situations involving money or property.

We would meet and have a long, healthy marriage together. Irene and I fervently believed we could help other people by being a model of what it means to keep being kind to each other in a family no matter what. Given our track record, we didn't know what our chances at success were, so we developed an emergency plan. This time we'd finally pull off our joint purpose…even if it meant working across the divide between heaven and Earth.

Choices like this are not so rare. Heaven often helps souls plan a tragedy to wake themselves up. So that's how I ended up dead in a ditch, leaving Irene to rely on her inner strength and knowing all by herself.

Moments of Recognition

In a way, we met in America before we met. Irene was a skinny, near-sighted beauty- in- waiting down in hot, sunny Florida, where she grew up. Her parents owned a few apartment buildings there in the years before real estate exploded near the University of Miami. Irene was a shy, intelligent sixteen-year-old who'd developed a crush on this young college student in one of her parents' apartment buildings. Passionate but inexperienced, she had no idea how the hell to approach this fellow and flirt with him.

My younger brother, Irv, was roommates with Errol, the guy on whom Irene had such a wild crush. Irene figured if she didn't have the nerve to approach Errol, maybe talking to his roommate might get her somewhere. So one day when Irv was sitting by the side of the pool at the apartment complex, she sidled over to him and began a faltering conversation. She asked him about school and the usual nonsense, and then, to break one of those deadly silent moments that terrify most adolescents, she asked, "Do you have any brothers or sisters?"

Irv, God bless him, said, "Yeah, I've got a brother up in New Jersey with a wife and kid. He's in real estate."

Now, even as unaware as she was about past lives or heavenly planning, this was a moment Irene remembers to this day. When Irv mentioned my name, she felt an electric current move from the base of her spine right up into her heart. The way she tells it, the current was so strong it almost jolted her right out of her skin.

And that is an example of divine intervention. Up in heaven, our angels were cheering and wiping their proverbial brows with relief. Our initial hook up had happened, and the next steps to bring us together could now go forward. Irene would remember the name Weinberg for sure and, hopefully, also the fact that I was in real estate. These would be wake-up calls for her later in life when we actually met, like heavenly seeds planted to help activate her soul memory when we finally crossed paths this time around.

Irene and I finally met as friends fourteen years later. I did a real-estate deal with her first husband, and we watched each other go through the hell of modern divorce. The reason Irene and I weren't able to find one another before marrying others was because our careful heavenly plans were no match for the levels of personal suffering both Irene and I endured as we grew, which is just another example of how life on Earth can mess with even the best of what a soul can hope for.

Irene left her husband very shortly after she had her son, Matthew, because her husband was too wounded from a painful childhood to sustain a healthy relationship with either her or their son. Three months later, I left my wife after years of misunderstanding and pain. Our disagreements had finally escalated into a daily life that was tearing our children apart. During this time, Irene and I gave each other the courage we needed to release the past and move into the present.

Since the day we'd first met, I'd thought Irene was something else—a little shy maybe, and a little more structured than I was comfortable with, but I couldn't get away from a feeling of always wanting her near me whenever I saw her.

Finally, living with my feelings stuffed beneath the surface wasn't enough. It was time to do something about it. When both of us were newly separated, we spent an afternoon together helping each other with errands. At the end of the day, the kids were playing in my house while Irene and I talked in the kitchen. She had some outfit on that had been driving me nuts all day. I'd been watching the way she moved and breathed. I'd been mesmerized by the pulse beating in her neck. Before I knew it, I had her in my arms, and I was kissing her like I had never, ever kissed anyone before—deep and sweet and soul- searching.

Irene was taken totally by surprise. Being the soul of rectitude, she wouldn't ever have considered such a thing without a more formal declaration between the two of us. This time, though, she decided on an impulse to kiss me right back, meeting me in that moment with all the passion and power of her whole being. I thought I was going to explode right there in the kitchen. I'd never felt such heat, such a magnetic pull, in all the days of my life.

After that we couldn't stay away from each other. That was it. If we were together in a room at all, we were touching. When we were alone, forget it. We were lucky the bed didn't collapse from the force of how we loved each other. I was a middle-aged fellow who'd never known such love. It literally took me over. All I could think about was Irene, keeping my head above water in business, Irene, helping my kids survive their transitions, and Irene. The passion I felt for each of those concerns was enough to give me heart palpitations on a daily basis.

Irene was as gone as I was. Divorce was still new in those days, and for two recently separated people to get together like we did, with such obvious adoration of each other, was not considered socially appropriate behavior. Irene was stepping outside the mold and going against traditional society's dictates in order to love me. Never before in her life had she gone against the status quo. That alone should prove how gaga she was over me. We both had to put up with an enormous amount of risk and pain to be together.

People in our community, for example, spent a good deal of their time labeling us in nasty ways. And our ex-spouses? Oy, what a mess! Irene's first husband stopped functioning outright for a while, leaving her and Matthew alone to survive on her modest salary. And since there were issues with her family, she couldn't possibly turn to them for help. My sweet Irene was hanging out there like ripped underwear on a clothesline in a windstorm.

As for me, I had so many messes I could barely keep up. My first wife had hit the roof when I'd left, doing everything she could to make my life as difficult as possible: money, custody, trauma, drama, you name it. Irene and I never knew what was going to hit us next. If only I'd run in the other direction or stopped seeing Irene altogether, everything in my legal situation would immediately have calmed down. But I couldn't do it. I never even considered it. We were lovers in a battle zone choosing to focus on loving rather than on fighting, and becoming more and more deeply welded with every new challenge we met as a couple.

I remember one incident especially well. Irene's work sent her on buying trips to the Orient. She'd been gone for a good two weeks, and you know what an eternity two weeks can feel like when you're in love and apart from one another. While she was gone, one of my friends convinced me to go with him to this singles' place down in Florida.

People were going crazy: sleeping with each other at the drop of a hat, drinking to excess, stuffing cocaine up their noses at every opportunity. Mind you, these were middle-class professionals, people who should've known better. It didn't take me long to realize there is no place like home, and my home was Irene. Before this trip I had been aware of my constant physical desire for her, but now I was suddenly face to face with how few women like her there were in the world. She was honorable, passionate, and dependable and an incredible mother. Looking out at that sea of well-tanned fleshpots and those silly, middle-aged men acting like crazy teenagers made me appreciate Irene more than ever. I'd never known a woman capable of such open surrender.

She loved my earthy, powerful body with a complete and unconditional delight. In the face of all that empty connecting going on in that singles' scene, I suddenly saw the full extent of the connection Irene and I were growing. I saw the way our passion was supported by the framework of unspoken integrity we shared. Irene's beliefs about family, life, and the world were identical to mine. I'd never been able to articulate them, yet she daily embodied those values in the choices she made for us and our kids.

You've got the picture here: secular guy has moral awakening in Sodom and Gomorra. So what did I do with this profound and terrifying revelation? I hightailed it home, found the largest bouquet of flowers I could lay my hands on, and got myself over to meet Irene at the airport. The minute she set foot off the plane, I leapt—in my best flatfooted but hopefully romantic Jersey businessman style— over the turnstile. Irene *plotzed* at the sight of me...well, that and the fact that I almost landed right on top of her. Once she recovered, I took her in my arms and asked her to marry me. She agreed, and we went home and made love until there was almost nothing left of either one of us.

I don't want to leave you here with the impression that every moment of our first years together was a bed of roses, sweetness, and peace. We had plenty of good arguments at the beginning as we moved in together and started building a decent blended family. Sometimes it felt like our families were in the same shape France and England had been in after World War II: wounded and maimed but bravely rebuilding.

We had a time of it with the kids, that's for sure. Irene and I were virtual pioneers when we sought counseling for our children and ourselves. We agonized every day over how best to help them have reasonably normal childhoods. One argument we had about my son, Bruce, during our first year together was a watershed moment for us as a couple—one of those built-in wake-up calls from heaven meant to keep me on the right track despite my distractions.

Bruce was an extremely bright, creative kid who perceived the truth about the behavior of all the adults in his life with a maturity beyond his years. This is enough to make anyone a little off center. Add teenage male hormones and a very permissive middle-class culture into that mix, and you've got an accident waiting to happen. On the advice of a very good family psychologist, I placed Bruce in an excellent boarding school during the worst of my divorce troubles.

The idea was to keep him out of the battle zone and give him the structure he needed to survive his adolescence.

It worked beautifully for a full school year, with the end of that time coinciding with the first year I seriously dated Irene. He came to live with me for the summer. After not having the benefit of my fathering for over a year and seeing me madly in love with a new partner, Bruce began acting out. One night, having reached the end of my patience, I told Irene I'd decided to send him back to boarding school. She pitched a holy fit because she knew what it was like to be cut away from family in that way. For years after marrying her first husband, her father not only had cut her out of the family, he also had insisted the rest of her extended family cut her out as well. There was no way Irene was going to stand by and watch someone else be sent away.

On the night I lost it with Bruce, Irene really spoke her mind. "Saul, maybe it worked the first time, sending him away. But your life is different now. You have me. We're making a decent home together. I know how it hurts to be shut out. If we do that to Bruce now, as we begin to build our family, he will always feel like an out-sider. He's a beautiful, talented kid who's acting out the pain around him and inside him. My gut tells me that as difficult as he is right now, he needs our love, stability, and this family life more than anything. We can give this to him. I don't feel right about your sending him away. As much as I love you, Saul, this matters enough to me that if you do this, I will not be able to live with you."

I couldn't see what she was getting at—and to threaten to leave me over it, for crying out loud! All I knew was my kid was driving me nuts, and the whole thing was making me feel like a failure. But I trusted Irene. I knew she was right. I was so fed up with the whole thing, I did what any self-respecting male would do: I went out and sat in my car.

I must have sat there for a good hour and a half thinking every-thing through. Damn, it made me mad! I hated seeing my boy in so much pain. I wanted to help him more than anything in the world, and I couldn't bear the prospect of trying to help him and failing. So there I was, frustrated, out in my car, and there Irene was, sweating bullets in the house. She'd taken the risk of losing me just to make a stand for my boy. *My* boy. What a woman.

My love for my son along with Irene's steadfast devotion to both Bruce and me finally won out. I went inside the house and made peace with her. Later that night I took her in my arms and made love to her like there was no tomorrow. I couldn't think of a better way to thank her. Beyond giving me back my son, she had succeeded in giving me one of the greatest gifts one human being can give another. She helped me stay on track with my soul purpose.

The Soul Purpose

Your soul purpose is the gift you came here to share with the human race, no matter how simple or grand it may seem. It also involves the personal relationship lessons you came here to learn this time around. Even when you don't consciously remember your soul purpose, you know it in the fiber of your being.

Given that your purpose is so central to the reason you came here at all, losing touch with it creates a marrow-deep feeling of alienation. Its absence can leave you vulnerable to behaving irresponsibly toward others. Unfortunately, many cultures and societies today seem almost rigged to help an individual *lose* the knowledge of his or her soul purpose. I'm talking about things like poverty, selfish abundance, racism, sexism, classism, and child abuse. Forces like these run rampant in the world today, and it takes a firm commitment to the truer, often harder path of staying open to the *real* you, to the real reason you incarnated in the first place. But rather than focusing on the importance of a soul purpose, I thought it would be more helpful to offer a practical way or two of learning to recognize that honest path.

Often you know you've strayed from your purpose only when you find a deadening, lonely alienation in your life that you can't chalk up to family, business, or social problems. In recognition of how easy it is to get lost from your soul purpose here on Earth, heaven builds all kinds of signposts and a variety of wake-up calls into your life to help you find yourself so you can find love and complete your soul purpose. Some of these markers are not only helpful, they're also easy and even fun. They might come in the form of a scholarship you unexpectedly get, or you might fall in love with someone special. Some of the not-so-fun ones are more like playing the coyote in a Road Runner cartoon: you survive, but you're temporarily toasted or flattened from the force of the impact.

These more difficult signs might include losing your job suddenly and being forced to find a whole new line of work. Or you might one day find your spouse has just dumped you. Sometimes these situations are plain bad luck or crazy human cruelty, but other times they are doors that heaven has built into your life to help you move in the direction of manifesting your soul purpose.

"Yeah, but how do you know which is craziness and which is heavenly inspiration?" I hear you asking, and that's a very good question. The answer has to do with learning how to sit quietly and breathe consciously in the middle of any crisis.

Of course when you're in the middle of a crisis, the only thing you can be certain of is a lot of trembling and panic. Lots of adrenaline pumping and guts quaking, no doubt about it. But it *is* possible that even during the first shock of losing a loved one, a job, your financial security, or whatever, you *can* take some time every day to breathe and to hope.

Your breathing on Earth is connected to God – a simple fact you don't realize until you no longer have lungs with which to breathe. Every time you inhale and exhale, you are receiving the heartbeat of the loving Source into your lungs. This loving radiance pulses into your bloodstream, your vital organs, your muscles, tissues, and bones and on into your neurophysiological processes. I realize this is a pretty revolutionary concept, but it's honest: if you rest in your breathing at any time in your busy day, you are actually allowing our loving Source to give you inspiration, strength, and good practical thoughts about living a healthy life.

When it's a legitimate crisis due to someone else's craziness or life's random cruelties, what you'll feel rising up in your gut when you quiet your rage, pain, and fear is a pure, heartfelt cry for help. That's right—a simple, unmistakable "help me!"

Now, if you have what it takes to sit inside that need for help and not *panic*, you might feel a prayer coming. Or maybe a detailed, practical list of what you need to help you survive your crisis might rise to the surface. If you shout these needs long enough at heaven, and you do your best to survive until help arrives, help *will* come in some form. I guarantee it. The trick is in breathing, staying centered, continuing to ask for help, and moving toward that help no matter what.

When the crisis you're faced with is actually heaven nudging you toward a soul purpose, however, you'll receive a different message when you get quiet. Under your fear, rage, and pain, you'll feel a sense of peace—a sense that there's something oddly right about this.

Now, there's no question that some of these nudges could come with a hell of a lot less pain and uncertainty. They'd sure be easier to read and recognize if they did, wouldn't they? Not to mention the fact that each of us is frequently guilty of actions that land us in the muck in the first place. But no matter how bad you feel, either because of the pain or any residual guilt, ask yourself—again, in that silence—if you don't also feel there's something kind of okay about this present emptiness. Could it be you actually feel some degree of excitement about the freedom this loss has given you?

The trick here is to breathe, to stay centered, and to try to let your soul purpose—that sense of what gives life the most meaning for you—rise to the surface. It may take weeks, and you'll have to keep making decisions in order to survive in the meantime, but even ten minutes a day of being quiet can make a difference. If you can just sit quietly in church, in temple, or in your car for ten minutes a day during this trying time, you'll give your soul purpose permission to be more present.

That moment with Bruce and Irene is a great example of heaven's helping me in this way. My soul purpose was to create a model family life based in living love as a decent, kind behavior. My divorce and business pressures had caused me so much fear and pain, I'd been willing to let my own kid go just to get a little relief. In Bruce's acting out and in Irene's integrity, I was being sent a nudge.

You see, Irene and I couldn't be a model for others if we were untrue with each other and our children. So together we began taking the necessary trial-and-error steps to balance everyone's needs on a daily basis. This was the core of our joint soul purpose, and it was hard, often brutal work. We wouldn't see the rewards of our efforts for quite a few years to come, but a deep knowing that we were doing the right thing reassured us over and over again. Looking back, I don't know how people keep going forward without a strong connection like that.

The good news is you don't have to do without it, once you've gotten quiet and clear enough to have that knowing work for you day after day. And the rewards that come once you know you're on the right path are unbelievable.

Unfortunately, a lot of painful living can go on before you become clear enough to start working through your pain and getting to the good stuff. Irene is an example of someone who has always tried to honor an inner truth even when she hasn't been completely sure what she is honoring. Making choices throughout her life that kept her open to love and possibilities enabled her to communicate with my soul after I died. She never let her lifetime of pain and suffering get in her way. It's the key to her strength, and it will be the key to her living a full, successful life without me. I know I've said it before, but I've just got to say it again: what a woman!

Irene's Epiphany

While I was growing up, my father, Jack, ruled our house with domineering looks and an ever-ready strap. Being stricken with polio at the age of five had left him filled with rage at his mother, specifically, and at life in general. The rage toward his mother started because she blamed him for contracting the disease while he played with the little girl upstairs. It was true he'd gotten the polio that way, but no one at the time knew she was infected since she'd only exhibited the milder cold-like symptoms. That truth didn't matter, though; his mother blamed *him*.

My own mother was too afraid to stand up to my father, and my two younger brothers and I didn't dare move a muscle without his permission. In between nightly prayers asking God to protect us from him and his rage, I tried to focus on the things in my life I knew were true blessings. Like school, which I loved, and my violin lessons, and the fact that most of my teachers were genuinely caring. All in all, it seemed as if God was doing the best that could be done for me—under the circumstances anyway.

Which was why I got it in my head that I just had to go to Hebrew school. It seemed like a real act of love and gratitude toward God to go through the Jewish ritual of a Bat Mitzvah and be welcomed as a daughter of the commandment. Normally, boys attended Hebrew school in order to become a Bar Mitzvah, "a son of the commandment," when they turned thirteen. It wasn't going to be easy to get my father's permission or the extra money needed to attend Hebrew school, but I was determined. I summoned up my courage and, miraculously, prevailed.

Getting this opportunity reinforced my belief that God really did hear my prayers. On the appointed Bat Mitzvah day, I sang and prayed my heart out for God, my family, and myself. That day held the extra blessing of a small miracle so precious, the memory of it helped me accept those messages I heard around the time my Saul died.

The Bat Mitzvah service went great, and after it ended everyone met for food, wine, and conversation in a reception area just outside the sanctuary. Standing in the crowd, beaming with joy, I watched an old man slowly approach me. We lived in a small community, and I had never seen him before. As he got closer to me, he motioned for everyone in the crowd to quiet down. I could tell by the reactions to his presence that no one in the room knew who he was either or even where he had come from. Once he'd shushed everyone, he began speaking loudly to us all.

"This little girl taught me a lesson today. I sat in this synagogue expecting to laugh. I did not believe a girl had the right to participate in a ceremony like this. But in my ninety years of life, I have never heard a *boy* pray with as much conviction and faith as Irene did today." He paused for a moment to put his hands on my head before continuing. "May God bless you as you have been a blessing to all of us today. May God grant you a full and good life. May your life be filled with meaning, and may it be as special as you are." Then he left the synagogue. As far as I know, no one ever saw him again.

Unfortunately, this kind of rewarding community recognition was short-lived. Life as a teenager boiled down to trying to be as perfect as possible in order to survive the angst at home. I excelled in my studies, performed well in the school orchestra, dated very little, and did what I could to keep the peace. I counted down the days until I could get away to college, but my father thwarted me once again by forbidding me to live away at school. When he closed this door on me, I ended up at a college near home, but shortly after graduating, I opened another door on my own.

I accepted the marriage proposal of a man I'd met on a blind date. We hadn't known each other long, and all we had in common were our Jewish faith and a shared sense of anger and injustice at the world. That didn't matter: my main goal was getting out of that house.

And get out I did. My new husband and I lived near my parents in South Florida, which turned out to be nowhere near far enough away. We all fought constantly. The battles got so intense that we decided we'd better put a lot more distance between them and us. It was a smart move survival-wise, but leaving Miami for New Jersey would end up costing me all communication with my family for long periods of time. And it wasn't just my parents I lost. My relationships with my brothers also got caught in the crossfire more than once over the next twenty-three years. Ex-communication was my punishment for growing up and getting out; even distant relatives were told not to have anything to do with me.

Tears came every day for months. Despite my grief, though, I noticed a seed of determination growing inside me—a determination to survive, to be sustained. I rooted that precious seed by saying to myself over and over, "I will not let this take me down. I will not apologize for a sin I didn't commit."

Looking back, I can see the ways heaven was there for me during my worst moments. Like the time I got a letter from my parents shortly after leaving Florida. In it, they said that since I had violated the commandment to honor thy father and mother, in their eyes I was no longer a daughter to them. Their words made me feel erased and totally alone. Except for God. In that lonely moment, I chose to embrace my faith and hold steady to my vow of never repeating the selfish, raging behavior of my father. That decision kept me walking forward to a place of healing.

I eventually got my wounded butt to therapy, which turned out to be the kindest thing I'd ever done for myself. In that office, I was witnessed and attended to. Someone actually wanted to see my suffering stop—what a revolutionary concept *that* was! Through the therapy, I was able to honor the importance of having been a good enough daughter and a faithful, devoted wife. Once I took that step, I could see how getting married to get out was an exchange of one suffocating experience for another.

Next, I began to see how our beautiful nine-month old son was already beginning to suffer at the hands of our unhealthy marriage. So I gathered up my faith, my determination, and my boy, and I started over once again. My job as a buyer for Macy's provided me with enough money to make this move on my own and get great childcare for Matthew. It would be from this humble, temporary home that I would date and later marry my greatest miracle of all: my Saulie.

When Saul and I married, there was a sweetness and consistency in the way we loved each other that carried us through our eighteen years together—simple, precious moments connecting us in every-day life like a beautiful string of pearls. I can remember so clearly the image of Saul *tummeling and pacing* with the phone over one of his many real-estate deals. As he did so, I would pass by and gently touch his arm to let him know I was with him. In response, his arm would encircle me as he kissed my head while keeping the rhythm of his negotiations going.

We also stayed connected by helping each other in countless small ways. One of my favorites always happened after we had com-pany. We did a lot of entertaining for business and family, and there was always cleaning up to do after everyone went home. Now, my guy was not the kind who would ever leave his wife alone with the cleaning up. In fact, he'd put on his "kiss the cook" apron, grab a dish towel, and chat and laugh with me while we put the house back in order-- together. With his hands in soapy water, he'd lean closer to me and, smiling broadly, say, "You think cleaning dishes with me is good? Wait 'til I get you upstairs. I can't wait to get my hands all over you." Now that's what I call foreplay!

Saul's deepest connection to me, though, had everything to do with who he was, not just what he did for and with me. The core reason I loved Saul was I had never known another human being as kind, loving, and filled with integrity throughout his whole being as Saulie was. He truly was my heart.

Before my memories start sounding like a testimonial to Saul and what a saint he was, I want the record set straight: he could also be a pain in the tush at times. I can't for the life of me remember what one particularly good argument we had was about, but I'll never forget how we stood and ranted at each other from opposite ends of our bedroom. The intensity we brought to those arguments was only matched by our passion for each other. And thank God for that mutual magnetic pull, because it helped move us toward compromise on thorny issues like ex-spouses, in-laws, business crises, and stepchildren.

But this one time, we could not seem to find that comfortable middle ground. We were both standing firm with our separate opinions when the front doorbell rang. We both tried leaving the bedroom to answer it, but we reached the door at the same time and jammed up like Keystone Cops. We looked at each other, laughed out loud, and fell into each other's arms. A long, passionate kiss got us away from the argument and into our bed with everything forgotten...including ever seeing who was at the door.

If leaving my family of origin behind, getting divorced and remarrying were not big enough events to navigate, becoming a custodial stepparent to my two teenaged stepchildren totally topped them all. Especially my stepdaughter, Sandi. She'd been through the hell of her parents' divorce and ended up in our custody—for her own safety, mind you -- but it was all totally against her own choice. She loved her father very much, but, at the same time, she was torn by a fierce loyalty to her mother that wouldn't allow her to accept my son Matthew and me without interfering with that loyalty. Her first words to me the day she moved into our new home were, "Let's get this straight between us. I hate you, and I hate your kid. So stay out of my face."

I understood that she was speaking from her pain and confusion, but it still hurt to hear her say it and it was just the thing to get my butt right back into therapy. I told my counselor, "I don't know how to do this, but this kid is going to come out of my home whole and my marriage is going to thrive if I have to rebuild myself, cell by cell, to make it happen." This marked the beginning of a counseling marathon. I attended individual sessions while Saul participated weekly in group therapy. We did so much counseling that I remember one day saying, "Saulie, are we husband and wife or a therapy team? When do we hang out our shingle, for God's sake?"

The night before Sandi's wedding, she gave me a gift so wonderful it made all the struggles with our kids worth it. While taking a car ride to ease our pre-wedding jitters, Sandi said to me, "Irene, you know I've tried to break up you and Dad from the day I came to live with you. I'm so glad I didn't succeed. I would never have known what a truly good marriage is if I hadn't lived with you two."

I was stunned. *My God*, I thought. *I can't believe I lived to hear this before I went senile.*

The truth is, our life was filled with these kinds of rewards, so many that I had a hard time picking the best ones to use in this book. But one I knew I'd include was the memory of my son's Bar Mitzvah, because it was an incredible experience. It was one of Saul's favorite memories too. We relived the joy of that day more than once during the last years of his life.

Of course, I was proud of my son -- but that was the only part of the celebration that came easily. And though I love throwing a great party, we had a ton of family politics and community maneuvering to deal with as we planned it. I'm glad we were able to pull the event off with our integrity intact, but I'd like to add that as nice a phrase as *blended family* is, the truth is more like chopped liver: you might all end up together on the same plate, but everybody gets pounded in the process.

We had to make sure Bruce and Sandi were happy. We had to make sure my ex-husband and his new wife were happy, and we had to make sure our friends and every member of our extended families played some active part. Because of the impact this day would have on Matt, Saul and I committed ourselves to making this a truly bonding, loving event.

The day of celebration finally arrived. The hall was dressed to the nines, and so were we. It was so rewarding to see everyone getting along peacefully. I couldn't think of a better gift to give my son.

As Saul and I stood on the bimah with Matthew and the rabbi, I watched my dear Saul place his hand on Matthew's head and look down at him. There was such love in his face for this boy he had raised as his own. Just then he looked over at his two kids. I did too, and it choked me up to see them smiling at my Matthew with real love and warmth.

We all ate, drank, lit candles, and danced. When my turn came to get carried in the chair and hoisted high during the Hora, I felt absolutely triumphant. I spread my arms wide, delirious with joy as people carried me around the room, laughing, swaying, and clapping their hands. We'd done it, and it was magnificent. Thank God.

These skills I learned while blending my family would later open the door to repairing the damage between my parents and me.

It all started at a craft show. I was drawn to a table displaying information about the Jersey Battered Women's Service. They were looking for volunteers. When I read the brochure about the signs of battering, I began to see my family as a clear example of that dynamic. Given my history, I really believed I could be of help to others, so I volunteered.

During the six weeks of intensive education and skills practice, I opened up and shared the pain of my own childhood. I was totally blown away as I began to feel compassion for my father, which led me toward letting go of my victim status and beginning to move on.

A year later, I got a phone call from my mother, telling me that my father had had a stroke. He'd given her permission to call and tell me about it. Though my initial reaction to her news was to think, *So long, Dad. Don't let the door to heaven hit you in the ass on the way out,* what I said was, "Mom, you know how I feel about Dad."

Her response surprised me almost as much as her phone call. "Yes, I do know. Growing up in our home was very grim." I was utterly amazed by her honesty. I filled her in on all the therapy I'd waded through. I told her about my volunteer work on the hotline.

"Mom," I said truthfully, "if you want to work on a relationship with me, you're going to have to know right up front that I no longer pretzel myself to be loved by anyone. If I can't speak my truth to you, I won't speak to you at all. You've destroyed the trust between us. You've gone back on your word to me too many times. You're going to have to travel a long way to reconnect with me, but I still love you, and I'm willing to try if you are."

The conversations that followed were so powerful, my mother ended up going into counseling herself. For someone of her generation, this was amazing, and it gave me tremendous respect for her. Slowly, my brothers began extending themselves to her, too, which brought her the additional blessing of reuniting with all her grandchildren, some of whom she had not seen for up to ten years.

During the next five years, my father became more and more ill. I thought about connecting with him, but his personality hadn't changed and the hurtful memories were still too strong. A few years before he died, I wrote my father a letter in which I told him that I knew he'd always loved me but hadn't been able to express that love to me. I told him how hard growing up with him had been, and I ended by wishing him comfort and ease on the hard road he had ahead of him.

My mother told me my father cried when she read him my letter. She kept it and re-read it to him a few times before he died, and each time he cried. I had let him off the hook; in so doing, I had empowered myself. No longer invested in holding onto the pain, I was now finally moving on.

Saul's Healing

Up here in heaven, I sing a song of celebration for every person who fought for good laws, worked hard to create plenty in the new world, or sacrificed his or her own life to help others accomplish the miracle Irene has just shared with you. Because this is how the human race moves forward: step by aching step, generation by faltering generation, sometimes falling so far back we have to start over again but always with the soul remembering that love can overcome.

It is possible to choose kindness and strength this time around. These earthly moments of inspired goodness are among the fundamental reasons we are born at all, because only on this planet can the manifest expression of heaven's love reach full fruition. Heaven forever seeks to bring the fullness of love to fruition on Earth, which is exactly what I felt at young Matt's Bar Mitzvah. His bright, young face and the earnest way he did his part made my heart burst with love. With Irene by my side, and seeing how Bruce and Sandi were fully accepting Matthew as their family, I felt complete.

This became engraved on my soul. When I crossed over, it was this memory that helped me regain total awareness of my soul purpose. When that happened, my angels knew I was ready to learn about the history of life and how each one of us fits into it.

I was brought to a physical setting I would've thought was nuts when I was alive, but completely delighted my eternal soul. This environment wasn't made up of my earthly memories like some of the stuff I'd seen on my tour. This place exists in heaven, and thank God it does.

Its architecture is amazing. The columns are tree trunks, and the roof is made of leaves. It's always sunny and warm, with the sun dappling an intricately- flagged stone floor in beautiful, shifting patterns. There are comfortable, hand-carved benches everywhere, some in groups or circles, some alone.

Souls from all races and cultures gather here to listen to a very special group of elders who have attained eternal wisdom during all different time periods: pre-history, Biblical times, the Middle Ages, and the present. It is the most fabulous pool of human experience you could ever hope to join.

This group of souls holds wisdom about every practical area of daily life, from economics to psychology, from architecture to art. These keepers of wisdom take different forms. Some lived as Native American medicine people, some as black Appalachian mid-wives, some even Nobel scientists. Their soul purposes are to share the wisdom of the ages with souls returning to heaven and preparing to return to Earth.

I have to say that other than making love to Irene for hours on end, this learning place is my true idea of heaven itself. There is nothing like the glory of being among them all, sharing wisdom, heartfelt prayers of gratitude, hope, and longing for the whole human race.

I was allowed the honor of sitting with the archetypal wisdom keepers who'd lived lives devoted to service in marriage and family. I discussed the origins of family through clans and tribes, including the concepts of monogamy and marriage.

The elders asked me to share what I knew about the changes occurring in family life across middle-class America. They wanted to know if I felt that all the distressing abuses they were witnessing were as dangerous as they appeared to be.

I told them that as bad as they thought it looked from up here, down there it was actually worse. I explained that seeing the potential for these crises was why I'd chosen to be a real estate developer, which was work that really went against my grain. I took it on only because so much of what's wrong in the world is due to abundance being in the wrong hands. I believed some of that abundance needed to be in the hands of simple, loving people before it could start doing some good. I also believed most families needed a solid level of material comfort to give them the strength to behave well to each other. It was no guarantee, and it wasn't the only solution, but it did make a difference.

The abundance I created buffered my family and gave us the tools we needed to love each other well. Providing the world with a model of healthy family abundance had almost wounded my soul to the core. Now that I was healing, I felt an urgency to complete Irene's and my joint soul purpose, which had been interrupted by my death. Seeing I was ready, my angels once again placed me into the loving hands of my mother.

The environment was a kitchen this time, complete with cookie jars and a teapot on the counter. Sunlight flooded through the windows, and a table in the middle of the room was loaded with sandwiches. I sat down, and my mom fed me a huge lunch with hot tea. In this incredibly nourishing environment, I felt the power of the imbalance I'd lived with ever since my mother's death had left me alone and at the mercy of my father's craziness. That level of pain had placed a wall around my heart—a wall that had opened only in some of the sweetest moments of joy I'd known in my life with Irene and the kids.

In this heavenly kitchen, I saw how I had missed too many opportunities to touch the faces and hands of my loved ones with joy and an open heart. I'd been so distracted by my attachment to accomplishing my purpose and so filled with such a lack of faith that I hadn't taken the time to sit and witness my own dear ones completely. Even in moments of great familial disagreement, there had been missed opportunities to stop, sit, look across the table at them, and say, "I love you."

Now, don't get me wrong here: it wasn't like I had been some cranky old fart living off in a cabin by myself when I had been alive. I had been a very loving man. But through this healing, I saw how the pain had shut off my capacity to give and receive love fully.

As I sat there being fed corned-beef sandwiches, Oreo cookies, and hot tea, I took a moment to look upon my mother's face, pained over having left me so early in my life. In her eyes, however, I saw pure, unconditional love. Her expression radiated the way she'd loved me no matter who I was and no matter what I'd ever done. I was her precious little one, and finally I knew it.

Just then the room began to dissolve, and Belle became the Creator. I instantly made the connection that our spouses, mothers and fathers, sisters and brothers, kin, colleagues, and friends are the eyes of the Creator looking upon us with love. I saw the many instances where I'd received and given this love, but they were less poignant in that moment than the soul-deep awareness of any opportunities I had missed.

With this greater vision before me, my soul truly and fully woke up. This was when I said, "Aha! I remember now! I have a greater purpose here that I didn't finish." This I call my "eureka!" experience. Now I could see the beauty of how it all works right alongside the beauty of who and what I am within this whole. I realized what a fabulous human being I am (or was) and what a truly special soul I remain. I have gifts to give. I am filled with love and good intentions. I am bright, happy, and charming, and I deserve special care.

I realized I didn't have to stay committed to being an overworked and lonely real estate developer. I didn't have to stay attached to being a man who'd become too exhausted to love his wife with the true depth of fire and passion of which I was capable. I did not have to stay attached to the guilt of putting my children through a divorce. There was absolutely no good reason for me to have kept all that pain wrapped tightly around me like a tattered cloak. My love of whom and what I am was far more eternal than any mistakes I'd ever made.

And this is the basic truth I desperately want to share in this book, so listen carefully:

Yes, you've made horrible mistakes, even those of you guilty of the most severe crimes against humanity. Yes, you have to stop being destructive and get help. But yes, you are a unique, precious, gorgeous, amazing, dazzling human being, and you are loved, and you are worthy of love.

"You know, Saul," an angel said, "we want you to remember another part of yourself. Do you remember you had another goal to achieve in this last lifetime?"

I told them I remembered that I was going to be an example of a man earning a good living and still being a good person.

"Yes, Saul," the angel said, "and do you remember you had another purpose to complete?"

I sat very quietly before saying, "Oh. Is that what all that bitterness was about in the last years of my life? Is that what all the suffocation was about?"

"Yes, that's what all your overeating was about."

The other purpose I still needed to pursue was about a unique agreement I had made to maintain cords of light connecting my soul with Irene's heart. These beautiful cords of glittering, starry light allow me to be in two places at once: in heaven and on Earth with Irene.

You see, heaven needed someone to hold this dual awareness in order to help them find a solution to the near-crisis level of earthly pain happening here, especially since World Wars I and II. Souls in unprecedented numbers have been coming to heaven tortured, abused, nuked. They are nearly untouchable in their pain, and something has to be done about it. I had agreed, as a soul before my recent New Jersey life, to be one of the first to keep my soul open to the heart of our loving Source and the earthly pain at the same time. In this way a door would open through me that would allow our Creator to feel in a new way what's going on in people's souls on Earth that enables them to do such horrible things to each other. Once heaven saw it through me and that handful of pioneers, some answers could hopefully be found.

I remembered God saying to me, "Saul, you're an ordinary guy who will feel all that pain. Heaven has watched you get trashed more than once. We do not want anyone getting trashed anymore. Jesus was sent, and Gandhi, Harriet Tubman, Eleanor Roosevelt, Native American shamans, and countless others, most of whom unfortunately were martyred in great suffering before achieving their chosen intentions of stopping the level of human cruelty engulfing the planet."

The conversation had ended with a request. "I need you to help me witness," my Creator had asked. "We are not asking you to suffer for love. I am asking you instead to live and witness love. Fall passionately in love. Love your children. Experience what happens in your soul when you are hurt beyond recall. Show me how a soul gets shut off from the body and brain just before performing a hurtful act, even one done by a loving and good parent or spouse. Come back and tell me. I want to understand. I want to help people stop themselves before they choose to act in these harmful ways."

That request had led me to sign up for perceiving the roots of pain that develop when people allow their hands and hearts and bodies to do bad things while their souls are still good. I remembered it was my service to share with God my experiences of how souls shut off from God and then try to touch as many people as possible with the understanding that the Creator loves you all personally.

That's what the Creator wants: to find a way to protect all of us against unnecessary cruelty. The Creator wants us to understand that love and help come through practical choices and the help of others.

My marriage to Irene was intended to be a teaching model for others to use in their attempts to live love as an active behavior toward each other. Unfortunately, I'd been so caught up in survival that I never turned to Irene for *real* solace or comfort. We did have a wonderful marriage, but in light of what I denied myself, I'd barely skimmed the surface of our ability to connect through lovemaking, talking, and enjoying life together. If I'd been able to take in the depth of our love fully, I would have been open enough to remember my deeper soul purpose while I was still in my mortal body.

I couldn't atone for what I'd neglected to do without a cooperation between heaven and Earth. I needed some way to communicate with Irene, but how was a former real estate developer who didn't believe in all that New Age baloney going to reach her from beyond the grave?

I had no idea. Irene and I had never believed in communicating with souls on the other side. Well, the joke was on me now. I had to have a way to break through Irene's beliefs and prejudices to get her to work with me because the truth was I was never going to be able to fulfill our soul purpose without her. I *needed* her to work with me in order to succeed.

You'll remember from the messages she'd received at the beginning of our story that heaven had already been preparing her. This gave me confidence it would all work out. I mean, if she was that receptive in the midst of losing me, she could do anything.

As my desire to work welled up inside me, I was transported to a large hall where there was a host of angelic beings. Thousands and thousands of angels were sitting quietly in rows going upward like bleachers in a stadium. There was an amazing stillness in the room as these angelic beings focused on healing. Their faces radiated love, kindness, concentration, and even pain. In that deep silence, I could see white, silver, gold, and icy blue radiant light emanating from every being.

I wish I had the words to do justice to the glorious tension made simultaneously of the absolute silence and the pristine, airy sound of a cappella voices that filled this room. Both elements were there for the single purpose of healing.

I stood, overcome with awe, as I listened beneath the high, cathedral-arched ceiling of this holy and wholly amazing place. Standing close to this host of angels let me know beyond a shadow of a doubt that I could depend on these mature, evolved beings to respond with love, strength, and courage in *any* circumstance. In order to help, these incredible beings need only one thing from you: for your heart, breath, and prayers to be open to them. They also need you to believe in them even when you're faced with evidence to the contrary.

For most of this last life, I did not believe in the presence of angelic beings. The idea just didn't make sense to me. Standing before them now, I could see what a mistake I had made. Here was a room full of angelic beings focused only on the suffering on Earth: on you and me and the starving child and the rapist and the doctors as they heal and the teachers as they teach. And to think I could've had access to all this during the years I had suffered. I just never took a moment to be still and open and let them in.

In that rare silence, I suddenly felt the penetrating awareness of the presence of our loving Source. As I tuned into the Creator, I saw a golden light in and around everything inside the hall. All the angelic beings—angels of every imaginable race—beamed along with this love-filled light.

The presence of these angels filled me with total ecstasy. Think about the nicest sunny, warm day you've ever known, the glorious feeling of falling in love for the first time, your very first orgasm, or the most amazing piece of chocolate cake ever. Do that and you'll begin to get a hint of what I'm talking about.

The golden-yellow light was just like the light filling those wondrous days Irene and I had shared in Italy. I felt the blessing of this penetrating light to the core of my soul. The penetration of the Creator literally goes into the cellular center of the soul. It is not a merging; it is a remembering of your origin, remembering that you came from the Source, that you will return to it, and that, while you were apart from it, you were never truly separated. The Source is your roots; it is your home.

When God gets inside you, you instantly know who you are. I started seeing the blueprint—the soul map, if you will—for my next birth, my next childhood, and what Irene and I would do together next.

The room filled with an angelic prayer going out to everyone on Earth. The core of this message was, "There are forces out of your control that are larger than you and seem much bigger than you can handle. But we are beaming love at you every day that is freely available. The way you invite this love, this aid, this balm, into your life is by breathing, by focusing on your heart chakra, and by cultivating your openness to this love. If you are open to it, no matter how you have suffered, you can find your way to relief."

What I want to stress is the quality and the attention of this love. Even if you do not feel or perceive it consciously, there are simple things you can do to be open to this love. Breathe, pray, meditate, and remember. Use all your inspiration and desire to heal, to open up, to wake up and keep searching for ways to heal on your own. One of the things heaven has learned through Irene and me since I died is that the harder Irene works through her grieving process, the more she provides heaven with new ideas for healing they never could have created without her. Heaven is seeking a new form of co-creative process. It has begun working for us, which means it can also work for anyone on Earth.

As it is said, God helps those who help themselves. I would offer the opposite as well: those who help themselves, help God.

It is a basic truth of my soul that I am Irene's soul mate. This means her soul and mine have a basic atomic structure that is so harmonious, it's like the notes to a song. I'm at my strongest, most loving, most intelligent, and most courageous when I'm in her presence. Just as one must have air to breathe, I need to be near my soul mate in order to truly thrive.

As her healing and growing progressed, Irene often wondered what the future might hold for us. So she arranged a session with me to satisfy her curiosity.

Love Never Dies

"**O**kay, Saul, now that I've sat here and listened to all this heavenly wisdom and agreed to help by starting this book, I've got a couple of questions I want to ask you."

"Shoot," he said.

"I promise not to get carried away here. But I'm trying to come up with questions I think readers might be interested in, and the first one that comes to mind after all you've told me is: what, in your opinion, is the best way a person can prepare for death and an easy crossing over?"

"Leave it to you to come up with a question that focuses on taking care of others, Irene. Actually it's a pretty simple thing.

"The key to helping yourself cross over well is living a life that's got some level of devotion—heartfelt, passionate devotion—that gives you both discipline and delight. Even if that devotion goes to caring for your Harley-Davidson or your stamp collection, if you live that devotion with a pure heart, you'll be building the skills you'll need to focus on the light and love that will carry you across the divide between heaven and Earth.

"The idea here is that if you practice this kind of self-love and focus in this safe, personal environment, then when you're either being wounded or you're wounding others, you get into the habit of looking to love when you need help. This sort of devotion enables you to live your life without worrying that you'll have to sacrifice your integrity, without worrying that your actions will be hurtful to others. By keeping love as your focal point, it's almost impossible to go wrong. And if you've gotten used to that, then, when you head into that dark tunnel, you'll instinctively know the easiest way to get home."

"I guess practice makes perfect in everything, huh, Saul?"

"No doubt about it, Irene. That's why we were such good lovers, huh, Cuz?"

"All right," I said, taking a quick look at some of the notes I'd made before this session. "I've been thinking—"

"Uh-oh."

"Stop kiddin' around, Saulie, and answer my question. I have all this information you've shared about how humans grow and change through all their incarnations and healing or whatever, but I'm wondering now if heaven changes along with us. And, if so, what do those changes look like?"

"That's tricky, because heaven really has been perfect for each time period it has addressed human history. Which means there's a lot of adjusting going on up here constantly. The changes are mostly about helping humans spark new growth, centering on whatever comes up while souls are in manifest form. Remember that free will and divine mystery always leave stuff up for grabs, and the most surprising ending can follow any action at any time.

"But mainly heaven is busy trying to find ways to help us without getting in our way. The point of earthly living is that every experience each of us has on the planet makes it possible for anyone else to take that same path. Everyone can become enlightened and everyone has the capacity to be totally destructive. What's different about right now in heaven, though, is that the level of crisis and suffering on Earth has reached such a peak, their main concern is how much more can be done to help without interfering with individual free will.

"Even the best-laid plans for a lifetime can go awry when someone else remains closed. It stops the help, and it stops that person from being able to participate in a plan even if he or she originally had been willing up in heaven. This includes soul mates. You could recognize a true love or a true friend, and they would be unable to see or feel that connection because they're so closed off—to heaven, to others, to themselves—that they're incapable of meeting you in that truth.

"So I guess the biggest change going on up here is that our loving Source is trying to get a better understanding of what it's really like for humans to suffer, because the old solution of rising above the pain isn't the answer anymore. What heaven wants souls on Earth to do is to pray, and in those prayers to complain more and more often. But it's not enough just to sit back and let yourself pray from a blocked or shut-off existence. People have to take active parts in healing the trauma and wounds they've suffered during one or a hundred lifetimes. Because the only way heaven can send help these days is in the form of practical human help through others. That's it. Faith is essential for co-creation. People should *absolutely* stand up and demand more help from heaven on a regular basis, but everybody's gotta know that's going to happen *only* if the person doing the demanding also puts as much energy and effort into healing his or her own issues at the same time.

"This newer way of looking at prayer and help should illustrate what a great responsibility a spiritual life is. Not only do you need to be a clean vessel in order to get help for yourself, you also need to be clean to help those around you. If people started cleaning up their individual acts, there would be fewer chances that soul mates would miss each other. Think of all the souls that would finally get chances to complete their soul purposes if everyone around them were dedicated to being open to God and their own healing. Man, what a great day to look forward to!"

I got goose bumps as he spoke. This conversation neatly led me to the question I was worried he'd be reluctant to answer. But I was determined.

"That's some real inspirational stuff, Saulie. Thanks. I know it'll be perfect for the book."

"That's what I'm here for."

I laughed. "Yeah, well, I'd like you to get a little more personal now. I've been listening for months to all this stuff about the human race and heavenly archetypes, and I want to take advantage of your unique place and ask you about us, about our future."

"Do you mean your future between now and when you die and I come get you?"

"No, I mean a future incarnation. I want a sneak peek. What do you say? Can you talk to me about where we'll be headed next time around?"

"Irene, you are so predictable! I knew you'd get impatient on me."

"Now, wait a minute!" I called out in my defense. "I defy you to find any human who wouldn't ask for a look into his or her future. Cool it, Saul!"

"All right, calm down. As long as you know that whatever I tell you lives only in the realm of potential, I'm willing to share a possible vision with you. But I need you to promise me you won't hold me to it."

"Would I do such a thing, Saulie?"

"Now, don't be a wise guy, Irene. You're only human, after all— you said it yourself. Just promise me you'll remember that—"

"That any action or belief can change any potential at any time, yeah, yeah. I promise. Stop stalling, and tell me about our future already!"

"The things I do for you....okay. One future lifetime, coming up:

"The way this all works is that most souls have both single life plans and an overarching soul blueprint that guides their eternal evolution. Your angels are basically in charge of this information, but if you ask them nicely enough -- and you've gotten clear of your pain -- you can sometimes get a glimpse of what the future might hold for you.

"Actually, getting clear and checking into your own knowing are probably much better ways since the blueprint lives right there inside you. It would make sense, don't you think, that your own knowing would be more accurate than the prophecy of any angel? After all, you live in that body. They don't.

"But since you've asked, and because I've never been any good at denying you anything, I'm going to pull a few celestial strings and show you a potential next chapter in our eternal love story.

"When you're finally old and tired enough to let go and die, I'll show up at your side and say something pithy like, 'Hi.' After you're done busting me about how long I've been gone, your angels will want to give you some time with family members before you begin your process of healing, growing, and evaluating the very full life you've just finished.

"I, on the other hand, will be chomping at the bit to reincarnate and be with you again because I'll already have been waiting so long. I can just hear what you'll say about that: 'Mellow out, Saul. I spent too many hours waiting for your and heaven's help while I lived alone without you. I'm not going back to Earth with you until I'm healed and rested enough for us to make choices that are safe and stable. No more mistakes!'

"You'll be right, of course, and, being the good Joe I am, I'll wait till you are ready. In the meantime, however, I'll be with my angels and our blueprint committee in order to put together the nuts and bolts of our next lifetime. And you can bet I'll be watching the situation on Earth to make sure we don't miss any chances to protect ourselves or our work when we return.

"When you're ready, we'll meet together with our angels to draw up our next blueprint. We'll do this in our usual way: lots of discussing and arguing. Both of us will already have met with our personal angels in order to design our individual blueprints. Yes, I'm sorry to say the procedure really is that complex. There are individual plans, sibling plans, couple plans, and on and on ad infinitum. Everything needs to have a harmony of timing and interconnection that makes a Rubik's Cube look simple by comparison. The worst part is that after you've gone through all this red tape to set the damn thing up, there is still *no guarantee* that all those planned connections and agreements will end up the way they were intended.

"Maybe, instead of telling the dry details this way, I should just let the story unfold after our plans have been made and we've hopefully arrived intact in the right bodies, the right lifetime, and the right neighborhood."

The Vision

I'm seeing a warm afternoon, late, toward evening. You know that time of day, when the sun gilds everything, and the world starts to look a little bit like heaven. The neighborhood is part of a planned community at some time near the middle of the twenty- fourth century. People have wised up about the state of the planet and are being much more careful to use alternative forms of energy, so this is what will come to be known as a *green neighborhood*.

The houses are built into the landscape and many have organic vegetable gardens growing on the roofs, in the yard, and along the street, which is not paved because it is used primarily for pedestrians walking to local schools and shops. In order to get to the larger city centers, people take solar-powered, flying public transportation. Streets like ours are places where children are clearly welcome and safe.

There is a community playground at the end of the street where parents and children are having dinner and relaxing at the end of the day. The conversation is filled with teasing and good listening, the kind of sharing that goes on between trusting people with common values. I can see a web of love and care stretching and flowing around the children and among the adults.

There's still trouble, though—it *is* Earth after all. I can hear some parents talking about how hard it was for their parents before them to survive the new addictions that have replaced drugs and alcohol. Some have lost both parents to the alienation disease that grows from spending too much time on the computer. These people lost basic emotional and communication skills, becoming empty vessels needing months of withdrawal time in rehabilitation facilities to learn how to relate to others without e-mail. Everyone is also worried about the continuing cycles of drought and bacterial infection that hit the planet regularly as a result of having taken far too long to stem the effects of global warming centuries ago.

There is peace, and there is happiness, but it is fragile and newly won. As I see these adults interacting, it is clear they are listening to each other with true empathy. Living love is now a common behavior, thank God.

Although the parent-child bond is paramount and lasting, the bonds between friends, elders, siblings, and spouses on Earth now still feel too fluid and changeable for my taste. I can see that Irene and I, being as truthful as we are, will have chosen to be born in this time to help people find that structure and cohesiveness. We will not, thank God, have to battle violence, hatred, and fear. We will have to battle ambivalence and lethargy, but I'm all for that. As long as I don't get signed up for any more extended separations or pogroms, and as long as I never, *ever* have to watch Irene suffer cruelty again, I'll be fine.

For her part, I know Irene will also be happy as long as I don't leave in an untimely way and as long as she's allowed to fulfill her soul purpose from an early age without first having to write a book!

Back to the scene: There I am, flying across the jungle gym, hand over hand, whooping and hollering. I am seven years old, and I feel the world is my oyster and the neighborhood my kingdom. My name is Stephen, and I am watching everything going on in my small world while I play.

I'm not much to look at—a wiry boy with red hair, a big nose, and a shit-eating grin on my face almost all the time. My one redeeming feature is my sparkling, warm blue eyes. And I am a *scutch*: I tease everyone around me, especially the little girl who lives next door, Judea. She's a real pepper pot. I like that about her. I like her fire. I also like the ways she uses that spark to defend the little kids in the neighborhood when the playing sometimes gets too rough.

There's Judea now, riding her bike down to the playground. Her mother and father are walking down the street behind her. It's clear how in love they are with each other and how much they adore their little girl and her older brother, who tears along beside them on his own bike. Judea's dark, curly hair glistens in the sun, and her sweet, knobby knees are pumping that bicycle to beat the band. Her determination is clear. She will most likely be quite successful in helping even a group of amoebas attain cohesive structure.

I don't consciously know our future at that moment. We are both only seven after all. But something about the sun on her hair and her fierce drive touches me in an unexplainable way, making me feel overwhelmingly protective of her at the same time that I want to tease her until she begs for mercy, which I know she'll never do.

Suddenly her wheel hits a rock, and she is thrown from her bike. I am down off that jungle gym so fast, my hands are smoking. I run over to her and gently help her pick herself up. Her parents, aware of the bond between us, allow me to step in. As she gets to her feet, I look into her green eyes, and a shock moves through both of us. I feel my heart constrict as if I have lost and regained something unbearably precious all in the space of a moment. She looks at me with a calm knowing and a simple acceptance.

Then I pull her hair. She spits at me, and we run off to play. My parents join hers, and they sit together at a table under some trees and begin to lay out our dinner. Our parents enjoy a tight friendship as Judea and I grow together through the years.

School provides a nurturing and cohesive structure for kids these days. It is one of the wonderful, shining elements of our new society. The curriculum is a blast, and the teachers are loving and good. At this time in the future, education is a whole different kettle of fish. After the great Peace Act of 2201, when all the countries of the world agreed to allocate two-thirds of their defense budgets to health and education, public school became a luxury. We have all been surrounded by individual teachers and learning plans since we were toddlers. This has accelerated our learning to the point that as we enter adolescence, we're just completing our liberal-arts educational requirements and are ready to choose areas of concentration.

The part of school that used to be hard—the academic part—is now a piece of cake. What gives everyone trouble these days is wondering if they'll pass their conflict mediation and emotional processing requirements. *Learning to be Kind to Yourself 201* is one of the real killers; *Learning to Meet Your Own Needs Without Killing Others 304* is another. Many children have to repeat these classes two or three times before they get them right, but not even such a wonderful, human-centered curriculum is enough to keep our social fabric from unraveling under today's stresses. As we approach early adolescence and realize our world isn't ideal, Judea and I begin having discussions about how we can help.

When we reach the age of twelve, we'll decide our areas of concentration. It's then that I look at her and the world around me in a different way. Our elders recognize that both Judea's and my gifts will help our community become more cohesive, so they ask us to attend the school with concentration in the areas of family and faith. We attend this school for four years, and our relationship makes a transition from teasing and play to a competitive scholarly friendship. We need this to survive the rigors of our training. In order to be masters in the areas of family and faith, we have to do hours and hours of self-examination and soul discipline training. We have to be able to look unflinchingly at our own nastiest behaviors and the very real failings of our families. One of our most intense assignments is to go to all our family members and ask them what they would like to see change in the way we treat them.

My mother tells me she's sick of seeing me worry so much. Worrying is like breathing for me. I feel if I give up worrying, I might just roll over and die. There is so much real trouble in the world! If I don't worry about it, won't all the trouble just take over and crush everyone?

One of my instructors helps me with this one day. He's training me to notice the breathing patterns I fall into when I start to worry, and he's helping me create affirmations about believing that the world will survive. I don't get it, though. I just can't make that leap and relax my muscles and mind in order to let go.

One of the foundational beliefs of our school is the understanding that faith empowers action. My instructor cautions me that if I can't put my faith in our loving Source into action in a daily way, my channeling will be affected. You see, I have a gift for hearing angels that is very dear to me. I don't want that touched. Plus I'm really growing to love walking to school with Judea every day. There is no way I'm going to transfer to another school and interrupt that pleasure.

So on this particular day, I am open to a transformation. My teacher looks into my soul and says, "Stephen, think of it this way: Who are you to play God? Who put you in charge of the world? You are masking a need for control as compassion for the planet. How about starting with yourself, healing your own fears, then taking your gifts out into the world to help others?"

Well, that makes sense to me, and after I try this advice for a few days, I find I'm a lot more productive and relaxed. I learn to have practical thoughts about my training or my future work instead of feeling fear every ten minutes.

And that's when Judea begins to let me know in small ways that she thinks I'm something special. She volunteers to chant and study with me more often. She even asks me for help as she struggles through her training.

Judea has a lot more confidence about the world than I do, but part of her future work will involve teaching ritual and speaking about sacred texts. She's struggling with a daily fear that she isn't good enough, that no one will listen to her. Her soul history teacher has explained to her that she has had several past lives in which she lost her life or was punished for speaking truth. She tells Judea to breathe and remember that her soul can heal any blockage by taking in love in the present, but try as she might, Judea can't get her leftover fear out of her cells. I sit with her many afternoons and beam love and strength at her while she practices giving speeches. She finally learns to open her heart and let love pulse through her with every heartbeat while she's speaking. That helps her focus more on her desire to help than on her fear.

We grow very trusting after many months of helping each other like this. What makes our trust even stronger is the way our chanting and prayer class shows us how harmonious our souls are. Our prayer teacher sits with all of us on a regular basis, and she can see the colors of our souls as we chant.

I love the chanting. I have a decent voice, thank God. I don't think my classmates could stand my enthusiasm if I didn't. I feel such joy at opening my heart to the generations of people who created these chants. The beauty of their devotion in love and faith over thousands of years gives me so much pleasure, I almost can't stand it.

The only person in our class who chants with as much gusto as I do is Judea. There's just something about our voices that matches. Her soprano nestles clear and sure around the lilt of my tenor. Our teacher says when we chant, our souls both take on a golden turquoise hue that is beautiful to see.

Time passes. Judea and I are sixteen now, and as our futures become more clear to us, we begin knowing what we will mean to each other. Judea has just won a local competition in public speaking, and she's repeating her speech for our class. We're all sitting in the school's courtyard where there's a fountain in the center of a lovely stone sculpture. It's a warm, early summer day at the end of the semester. The sound of falling water and the late afternoon sun embrace all of us in a gentle glow. I'm sitting on one of the benches near the front, hoping to make a rubber mouth at Judea to distract her while she's showing off for everybody. I'm so proud of her, I can't think of a better way to express my pride than to try to upset her. But I become so lost in the beauty of her words, I end up sitting there and beaming at her, embarrassing myself completely. Fortunately this behavior ends up distracting her more than anything else I could have tried.

Judea's speech is about living love as an active behavior to yourself and others. Her point is that even though we have progressed from the horrible emotional cruelties of the dark ages of the late twenty-first century, there is still work to be done. As I sit there watching the sun play on the dark curls of her hair and watching the pulse beat gently in the silky skin of her throat, I'm struck so hard by an inspiration that I almost fall off of my bench.

I realize Judea and I could work together. We could join my spiritual understanding with her structured knowledge of the sacred word, and together we could teach others how to build a new global cohesiveness of peace and understanding. I don't know whether just to stay seated and cover up my hard-on or jump up and tell her the news right away.

At that very moment, she's saying love is eternal and is stronger than even the divide between heaven and Earth, according to a late twentieth century couple, Irene and Saul Weinberg. They had bridged the divide in order to reach each other and share heaven's wisdom with people through their love.

Now I can hardly wait until she's done talking. I jump up the minute she is and ask her if she will please, *please* take a walk with me.

"But Stephen," she says to me, "I want to be here with all my friends. I want to enjoy my celebration."

Thank God she sees something in my eyes that touches her heart because I don't know what I would have done if she'd said no. She agrees to come with me for just a few minutes. We go into the garden behind the school. I enthusiastically begin spilling out everything I've perceived about working with her. She looks at me as if I have lost my mind. Then I do what any self-respecting sixteen-year-old would do when faced with the choice between an erection and an argument: I gently but firmly take her in my arms.

I can't believe how good it feels to hold her. I almost melt into the softness of her body against mine. It feels as though I've been wanting to hold her for centuries. I am weak at the knees.

Judea smiles at me with great tenderness and pulls my face close to her own. I kiss her, very softly at first, because her lips feel so warm I could practically die. Then we dive into each other. When we come up for air, Judea looks into my eyes and says, "I have no idea what the heck you're talking about, but something tells me we have worked together and loved together before. I know deep inside me that taking this on with you is exactly right. I'll always be willing to help you, Stephen, because I will always love you."

I am utterly speechless now, which never happens, but I manage to say, "I love you, too, Judea. I love you so much I want to hold you, kiss you, be with you, and work with you for the rest of this lifetime and a thousand lifetimes more."

Sixteen Years Later

"Saul has to go. Many lessons will be learned by his death."
"He's not going to make it. You are."
"Be loving and kind to everyone."

When Saul died instantly next to me, the important lesson I immediately absorbed was that I have control over absolutely nothing except how I choose to handle life's challenges. This, along with other profound lessons I've learned in the sixteen years since the accident, has formed the core of who I now am, especially as a result of the third message I received: "Be loving and kind to everyone."

It took a lot of inner fortitude for me to gather my courage and come out with my book in 2001. I literally had not yet found my voice because there were people who were downright hostile to me when they first heard my story. Naturally this made me feel somewhat scared and anxious.

Today, shows like *The Long Island Medium* with well-known and popular Theresa Caputo as well as appearances by famous mediums like John Edward and James Van Praagh easily attest to the widespread, growing acceptance and belief in life after death. These mediums are exploring beliefs our ancestors held for thousands of years. The old is becoming new again as it continues to comfort and inspire a continually growing audience.

I was able to find my voice through my work with a gifted medium shortly after I published my book. As the opener for her "galleries," or group readings, I would tell my story -- an ideal vehicle that helped people feel comfortable with what they were about to experience. This unique window enabled me to see many deeply grieving people begin to heal as they became convinced their deceased loved ones were still present in their lives and their souls had indeed survived physical death.

An additional bonus I derived from telling my story at these galleries was finding out that most people did not consider me weird or wacky; but to the contrary, they were welcoming, believed me, and wanted to hear those messages of hope and wisdom. They told me that my story gave them an enhanced understanding of and perspective on life that triggered shifts within them, inspiring them to become better people.

It was heart wrenching to witness the panicked tears shed by people who were distraught over the terrible arguments they'd had or the unkind actions they had committed towards a now deceased person just before that person's death. The guilt they felt was palpable. And at times it was the opposite: I also witnessed the deceased apologizing to their loved ones on this side for that last fight, those last ugly hurtful words that had been spewed.

The message *"be loving and kind to everyone"* would once again echo within me as I was reminded that we must treat the people in our lives with love and kindness whenever possible. It's important to be mindful regarding what is said in the heat of an argument because those could be the last words you will ever speak to your loved one or ever hear from the one you dearly love.

Indeed, the night before he died, Saul hugged me and said, "I'm so lucky and thankful to have you in my life." Those cherished words will remain in my heart and nurture me for the rest of my life.

I also often heard the deceased tell their loved ones that it is more than okay to love again, and Saul has also transmitted that message to me. There appears to be no jealousy on the other side, as your deceased loved one knows he or she will be with you again and wants you to have happiness while you are still on your earthly journey.

Understanding and accepting this gave me the permission I needed to allow myself to enjoy some new romantic relationships in the years following Saul's death. Since these relationships did not evolve into a long-term commitment, I have continued to enjoy my life, welcome new experiences, keep the faith, and practice divine patience.

Immediately after the accident, I often cried over the seemingly insurmountable dramas I had inherited; they felt like tangled strands of spaghetti that needed to be separated and figured out in order for me to survive. There were the financial dramas, the business dramas, the angry, grieving stepchildren dramas, other relationship dramas, the physical dramas (I've had three surgeries to repair injuries from the accident), the drama of reconfiguring a new relationship with my son, my own grieving and loneliness drama, the new dating scene drama, and more. I was in tremendous pain, so I turned to trusted others to help me. I built what I began to call "my wagon train" of people who could offer me proper support—financial and business guidance, emotional support, spiritual support—and just plain wonderful, compassionate, wise, good friends and family members who loved me. They listened with love as I cried, vented, and eventually figured out how to separate those tangled strands of spaghetti in my life.

There was no way I could have done all that alone. The accident had taught me that I had a choice: to remain a victim of my life's new dramas and challenges or to separate from them, strive to overcome them, and begin to heal.

I decided to turn to a highly recommended life transition coach named Dr. Ange DiBenedetto to help me figure things out, work through my grief, and begin to construct a new solo life. Dr. Ange helped me find the courage to walk through many a new door while reminding me that I could always walk right back out if anything made me feel uncomfortable.

As I traversed the stages of grief, at times kicking and screaming in despair, I would often wonder, if grief was so hard for me—an enlightened, educated adult—to cope with and bear, how could a child handle it? So it seemed meant to be when I was invited to what was termed a *future search conference*, the goal of which was to explore the need for an organization to help children and their families cope with the death of loved ones. I subsequently became a founding board member of an organization that was formed to help grieving children and their families cope with bereavement and heal from loss through peer support overseen by trained facilitators and professionals.

This led me to a wonderful new healing organization which is now being created by an extraordinary, talented group of people who wish to help adults and children heal not just via peer support but also through a new dialogue about grief and life and death through the arts. I feel deep gratitude and joy to be a part of this incredible team dedicated to making profound differences in the lives of the grieving via drama, music, writing, art, and more.

Writing my book opened me to the concept of reincarnation. Newly aware that karmic repercussions can occur due to unresolved relationships, I decided to attempt to repair some of the worrisome relationships in my life before I crossed over. To help me accomplish this enormous feat, I added the amazing energetic, healing gifts of a very gifted spiritual healer named Seta Araz Shahinian to Dr. Ange's wise guidance and help. Armed with the newfound grit that came as a result of the healing work I was doing with both Dr. Ange and Seta, I inspired my mother to go to therapy so that she could understand what had happened to her and her children as a result of the intense emotional abuse we had all suffered through the years.

I will forever admire Mom, who was in her seventies, for being willing to be accountable and to open herself up to healing.

Mom, my two brothers, their wives, and I eventually worked with Dr. Ange to heal the fissures created by years of emotional abuse and abandonment. Through my work with Dr. Ange and Seta, I also became empowered to resuscitate a failed relationship with a beloved sister-in-law and detach with love from conflicted relationships with my stepchildren so we could later co-create new healthier relationships.

I could not have done a speck of any of this without the wisdom and support of these very excellent healers who became my allies in my upward climb, step by step, toward healing. It is more than okay to ask for help, as no one is meant to process alone. And each of us processes at our own unique, separate pace.

Some of the most poignant validations I have received in both galleries and private readings from mediums regarding the soul surviving death are very specific communications from my father. Dad must have had a very insightful life review when he got to the other side because I have never, ever asked to receive a message from him, yet he has often come through un-beckoned, humbly asking for my forgiveness. He has referred to himself as a wounded child in an adult body who constantly competed with his own children for my mother's attentions and affection and resented his children for taking her away from him. He now seems to understand fully how much he hurt his family members.

Dad has stated that he is around me and has often expressed thanks for all the personal healing work I have been doing because it appears that as I heal, he does also. So not only have I been able to heal along with my family members on this side, but our healing work is also helping my father on the other side. Talk about a profound blessing!

By the way, for those of you who do not want to see that person who hurt and abused you when it is time for you to cross over, a word of comfort: I've received word that my father will have to wait for my mother's permission to approach her when she gets there.

Good thing, because Mom jokes that if Dad is going to be meeting her when she crosses over, she's not going!

As I've continued my healing journey, I've chosen to give up outdated concepts that are no longer relevant to whom I now am. At times it has been difficult to change course, especially when loyalty to a tradition, an obligation, or a family pattern has hooked me to an attitude or idea that no longer feels true for me. I continue to do my healing work because I am motivated not to have to return lifetime after lifetime, attempting to learn the same lessons over and over again with the same people.

My work with Dr. Ange and Seta has also helped me form a new loving relationship with myself. I have learned that self-love is not some vain, narcissistic, ego-driven state. It is a state of mind wherein we value and cherish ourselves by both healing our issues and taking good care of our health as loving gestures to ourselves. Self-love gives us permission to receive love and all we desire. Without it, we continue to feel intrinsically unworthy.

Self-love is acknowledging that we are all flawed and that committing mistakes at certain times in our lives is inevitable, yet with self-love we are able to forgive ourselves for those mistakes, learn from them, and choose to evolve with awareness from them.

One thing is for sure: healing, and helping others to heal, is now a passion in my life. As with most of us, I am aware that I have become a never-ending work in progress that continues to unfold.

Filled with the wonder of it all, I am literally ready for the next chapter in my life. It's not every day one gets pulled from her car, her husband newly dead next to her, while hearing the words *"be loving and kind to everyone"* authoritatively trumpeting in her head. In that one amazing, humbling moment, I made a leap from being a non-believer in anything other than my traditional Jewish beliefs to surprise and gratitude for a spiritual awakening I would eventually identify as part of a divine plan between Saul and me, decided upon with the help of our spirit guides and angelic beings before we had once again embarked on a new lifetime together.

I have come to understand that Saul completed what he set out to do this time around, but I apparently still have much to accomplish to complete the soul growth I set in motion before I was born. With the help of Dr. Ange, Seta, healing essential oils, and other healing modalities, I've continued to clean my emotional, physical, and spiritual houses in order to make it easier for Spirit to work through me. This journey hasn't been easy, but now that I've travelled through the various dark tunnels of dysfunction, lessons to be learned, grief, letting go of the need to control, attaining a state of acceptance, forgiveness, letting go of suffering, and so much more, the relief I feel is palpable.

One of the greatest lessons I've learned on my spiritual journey concerns discernment. I often liken the gifts of seeing, hearing, and sensing Spirit to an incredible ability in art, music, math, sports, etc. Some people have these gifts and ignore them, and some people have them and choose to develop them further. Then it is up to them to transmit the messages they are hearing for you to you.

I've been privileged to experience the gifts of spiritual channels and healers who are emotionally healthy and filled with integrity, but I've also been told, "Saul's soul is going to be annihilated" when I didn't do something a medium wanted me to do. I have been negatively affected by the energetic assaults of people I have displeased when I have adhered to my own standards and morality, and I've witnessed a well-known celebrity in the spiritual world being arrogant and insensitive to someone working for him (so much for walking your talk by being loving and kind to everyone).

All of this has taught me not to give my power away to these people. Who says someone who can channel the other side is better or wiser than you are? Do you know what is going on in that person's head and heart, how intrinsically pure he or she is? Or the level of integrity to which he or she holds himself or herself accountable? Or what stories and burdens are still carried within that have yet to be cleaned up? Do you know how cloudy that person's filter is as he or she reads you and communicates with your deceased loved ones?

My advice, gleaned from both the good and bad experiences, is to find healers and mediums with good reputations for integrity. Go to a healer who has done his or her own healing work so the filter is clean and doesn't get in the way of your healing. And over time collect data. Does this person walk his or her talk? How does that person treat people imagined to be lesser than he or she is? Is this supposedly spiritual person simply marketing a niche concept for financial gain or transmitting sincerely from the heart a message or messages to help others heal? Does this person stay grounded, knowing with great humility and gratitude that he or she is a vessel for Spirit to work through, or does that person think he or she is all powerful and better than others due to his or her gift?

Is this supposedly spiritual person to whom you are giving your money and trust immersed in ego or truly on a mission as a light worker in this lifetime with gratitude, humility, and integrity?

Some of the people in my life were wonderful to me while I was wracked with pain and in turmoil, but when my life seemed to be transforming in a good way, some of these very same people turned on me in various ways, and our relationships became toxic. When healing issues had begun to change me, some people were attracted to and inspired by my new changes while others were repelled by them and seemed to resent my newfound independence and sense of empowerment. It felt like they wanted me to join them in their toxic swamps instead of joining me in the light.

My newly developing sense of self helped me separate from those relationships that were bringing me down in one way or another. My biggest challenge was not to interpret toxic affronts as personal attacks. I finally got that these assaults came from unhealed issues within certain people that I had apparently triggered in some way. I began to think of these people as some of my best teachers, making me much less needy for approval from everyone.

Thanks to continued healing, I can now release toxic people from my life with love. Letting go of these relationships that were intolerant of my newly transformed and enlightened self was imperative to maintaining my well-being, my new energy, and my overall health. After all, each of us is here in this school called life. Can it be that these underhanded, jealous, insensitive, or rude people are simply not that evolved yet? What right do we have to judge others when we have committed so many mistakes in this life as well as in past incarnations?

There are now new, positive, and good people in my life who share my optimism and appreciation for life's possibilities and synchronicities. I have found these people by staying open to new friendships and new ideas and not allowing myself to become stagnant, rigid, and set in my ways. I have chosen to surrender to the possibilities and path the universe is continuously guiding me toward.

As I took my first baby steps toward healing and then kept going, I learned I can focus on my dramas or choose to focus instead on using those dramas to bring me to healing. I've released negative thought patterns and blockages and have converted them into positive beliefs and behaviors, which has enabled me to be happy and joyful in many more of my present moments.

The primary difference between who I was prior to the accident and who I am now is that I am now a conscious human being who is aware there are karmic consequences to the words I choose to say and the actions I choose to take. I now know for sure that there is a greater meaning to this life I am living. As a reminder, we are in control of only our responses to the people, events, and situations that unfold in our lives. We can be empowered only when we assume responsibility for ourselves and all our thoughts, words, and deeds.

I now strive to be more present to how my daily choices affect others as well as myself. Living my life consciously has made me a better person to be around, not only for the benefit of others but for my own benefit as well. I've learned that in the same way nuclear radiation resulting from the tsunami in Japan is now spreading and affecting the whole world, kindness passed forward to many others reaches a magic tipping point that results in less violence, which energizes and enables people to live in a space of joy instead of a space of lack and disappointment.

I've seen firsthand how living love and kindness as a behavior has made an indelible, lasting impression upon the lives I've touched. It's also made an indelible, lasting impression upon me. This is a blessing for which I am deeply grateful. As we develop awareness and a willingness to impact others positively, we can consciously choose to be loving and kind. The recipient of love and kindness derives a sense of worthiness and validation as he or she receives the blessing we have chosen to give. Likewise the one who has given love and kindness derives a sense of joy and satisfaction for having nourished and empowered another's soul (not to mention that Spirit will regard this individual more favorably!).

In order to give love and kindness, one must first have love within himself or herself. The choice to give love generously serves to raise the vibration of the giver as well as the receiver, allowing for both to share and experience the highest frequency that exists, which is love. When an individual resonates with love, baser emotions and negativity cannot easily co-exist within that being; therefore love elevates us and purifies us as we are purged of our less-desirable traits. To exercise giving love is to heal oneself as well as others. The benefit is mutual.

As I continue to model what it is like to heal and grow from within, people whose lives I've touched have become inspired to heal and transform their lives also. We are all a part of the collective whole, influencing all that surrounds us. With great humility, I realize that I have become a mentor and role model to younger women whom I have come to know and love.

I now know for sure that my soul is my loving partner who planned my current life with the input of my angelic beings and spirit guides, all trusting that I would make good choices that would enable me to grow and evolve in this lifetime toward my highest and greatest good. I'm not expected to be perfect, and when I make mistakes I know the angelic beings and spirit guides unconditionally love me anyway. I continuously hope I will learn from my mistakes and continue to grow and evolve, knowing that I must still love myself and forgive myself no matter what.

I also know for sure there is a wonderful place to which I will return at the end of this lifetime and I will come back to learn new lessons and love again, hopefully with a lighter soul and a lighter heart.

Spirit will always unconditionally love and forgive me as I invoke divine grace, which is our Source's ability to forgive us and remove the burdens that encumber us. Remember, the only things we will take away from this world are our souls. When our souls evolve and learn the lessons they are intended to learn when we choose to incarnate in the physical vehicles we currently occupy, we have specific goals and objectives to achieve.

We pass on to the next level or the next grade only if we do our homework, choosing to be diligent in our awareness and discernment by holding ourselves accountable and responsible for our thoughts, words, and actions. The requirement for each soul to evolve spiritually is the reason for this physical incarnation.

We are on Earth. When we mess up, the next lifetime becomes only harder to bear. We are held accountable for all we speak, think, and do. Freedom from all burdens that weigh upon us can be achieved only with awareness and accountability and with the help of the ever-ready healing resources provided to each and every soul by our Source, including the grace of prayer.

Take the time to be introspective. The future of your soul is dependent upon your conscious choice to evolve. It's never a smooth journey. Like a toddler learning to walk, we will all take steps forward and backward, falling down and standing up again.

Most important is our simple choice to choose to heal and evolve.

What path will you choose to take this time around?

With deep gratitude, I wish you courage, and I wish you well.

Epilogue

I hope the story you've just read about Saul's and my timeless love for each other has given you comfort and ease as you journey toward home in this lifetime.

I will be forever thankful and humbled by the gift of this book and its wisdom in my life. I have learned that what we do in our lives on our spiritual journeys affects us all; as we change, we become changers, hopefully to the universal good.

If Saul and I can leave you with one thought, one significant impression, I hope it will be that life is meant to be lived consciously, with love and kindness not only to others but also to yourself.

Enjoy your present moments. Watch that sunset. Take that walk. Take good care of yourself. And be sure to see and love the people in your life. Let them know *often*, not only with your words but also through your behavior toward them, that you love and care about them.

May love light your life always.
From my heart,
Irene

About the Author

They Serve Bagels in Heaven: One Couple's Story of Love, Eternity, and the Cosmic Importance of Everyday Life begins with the amazing messages Irene Weinberg received from heaven during the tragic car accident that took her husband Saul's life.

Irene resides in Northern New Jersey, where she oversees business interests. She is a mother, a stepmother and a grandmother.

They Serve Bagels in Heaven: One Couple's Story of Love, Eternity, and the Cosmic Importance of Everyday Life can be ordered through www.amazon.com.

Referrals

Dr. Ange DiBenedetto

Using a Holistic Approach to Help You, Your Family, or Your Relationship to Heal, Grow, and Thrive

- Holistic Psychotherapist
- Trauma Specialist, Somatic Experiencing® Practitioner
- Wellness/Life Coach and Advocate
- Nutritional and Self-Care Counselor
- Electrotherapy Clinician for Pain Management

There are moments in your life when you need a compassionate and insightful psychotherapist to help you get to a better emotional place. Other times you need a caring, action-oriented coach who can guide, support, and hold you accountable to realize a specific goal or help you navigate an immediate challenge – or opportunity. And sometimes you need someone who is both a therapist and a coach.

Regardless of the challenge or need, Dr. Ange brings a holistic mind, body, and spirit approach to working with clients. Based on her 25 years of experience as a therapist and coach, Dr. Ange passionately believes that each person can change their lives personally and professionally. She enjoys giving her clients the support, understanding, and direction they need in all aspects of their lives.

Call Dr. Ange at 413.549.4145 for more information.
www.dr-ange.com
> Working both in-person and, if needed, over the phone:
> - Therapy for Individuals/Couples/Families
> - Coaching/ Mentoring/Advocacy
> - Family Repair For Adult Children and Aging Parents

Seta Araz Shahinian Seta@ehealings.com

Seta Araz Shahinian is a seasoned facilitator of the healing arts. She has pursued her education worldwide, expertly integrating all the knowledge she has acquired along with God given gifts and insights that are uniquely hers. She has delved far into the energetic world and has been instructed by Source, developing modalities and techniques that have been instrumental in bringing healing to countless souls since she first established her thriving practice in 2001. Time and again, she has proven that the solution to problems that are prevalent in many of us, lies within the energetic realm and that we must seek solutions beyond conventional therapies and interventions, if we are to truly succeed in overcoming our challenges and weaknesses.

Seta is a gifted channel for writing customized prayers needed to overcome any set of limitations, thereby empowering her clients with the tools and resources necessary to actively partake in their own healing, as they assume responsibility for themselves and develop a personal relationship with God. Seta is in the process of sharing the gift of prayer conveyed to her with all those who seek Divine assistance. These prayers are all Divinely channeled with the express purpose of bringing profound and effective healing to all those who are unable to personally benefit. You may access certain prayers, techniques and gain insight into profound truths revealed to Seta at Ehealings. com. The essentials of prayer, common mistakes made while praying, how to pray effectively and correctly, how prayers affect and alter us, what differentiates one person's prayer from another's are some of the questions Seta addresses. This information will be freely made available in early 2014 when Seta releases her Ehealings app.

As a conduit of Source, an instrument of healing and the Grace of God, Seta has been instructed and taught how to alter the bio-energy field, negating and eradicating the obstacles that prevent individuals from attaining their goals and living a fulfilling life. Her passion is to identify all of the obstacles, negative influences and patterns within the energetic blueprint that cumulatively contribute to people's inabilities in resolving their particular challenges. Seta is able to determine the nature of these burdens, be they karmic in nature, unresolved issues from past lives carried forward, vows, foreign negative energies, possession, curses, addictions, negative beliefs, sabotage patterns and a multitude of other factors that may contribute to dis-ease (the lack of ease within). She also specializes in co-dependency, reconstructing and repairing poorly developed or damaged aspects of the energetic anatomy.

In addition to her in-person and distance energy healing services, Seta has also conducted group healings for those searching for wisdom and the means of attaining greater overall health, balance and well-being in their daily lives. Seta deems it a privilege to be of service to those who seek assistance and is committed to alleviating needless suffering as a facilitator and conduit of the Divine.

In the future, extensive healings, highlighting specific goals, such as the eradication of curses, rewriting one's future, altering one's life path through the Grace of God, exorcism through prayer, allowing for abundance, forgiveness, addictions and many more will also be made available through her Ehealings app. You may contact Seta at **Seta@ehealings.com**. Seta works in Wyckoff, New Jersey and is available for both private and long distance healings.

Gina Marie McConeghy, CHES, Holistic Wellness Consultant Certified Clinical Aromatherapist

Gina Marie McConeghy uses her holistic coaching experience along with her vast knowledge of essential oils to help people integrate the healing properties of essential oils, including essential oil infused supplements, personal care products and healthy home solutions into their lives.

Essential Oils are natural aromatic compounds found in the seeds, bark, stems, roots, flowers and other parts of plants. Essential oils have been used throughout history in many cultures for their medicinal and therapeutic benefits. Modern trends towards more holistic approaches to self-care and growing scientific validation of alternative health practices are driving a rediscovery of the profound health benefits of essential oils, which can address many health concerns without side effects.

On an energetic level, essential oils are a conduit to spiritual enhancement, emotional release and healing, providing natural support for each person in the family, extended family, friends and also pets.

Gina's ability to teach others how to use essential oils empowers them to create deep friendships, healthier families, and healing communities.

For more information: Contact Gina McConeghy **gmcconeghy@ optonline.net Subject: Bagels and Essential Oils**

Arlette Cohen practices the Art of Jin Shin Jyutsu, an ancient modality that uses gentle touch to stimulate the flow of energy within the body, thus restoring balance and harmony. With the help of her angels she also uses guided imagery to take clients to a place of unconditional self-love, peace and limitless possibility. Arlette became aware of her intuitive insight into the spiritual world through her years of working as a Registered Nurse. She is inspired by the belief that we are all endowed with the ability to harmonize and balance ourselves: Spiritually, Mentally and Physically.
Arlette Cohen: arlettecohen@yahoo.com

Pamala Oslie

www.LifeColorsCity.com
auracolors@auracolors.com
805-687-6604

Author, radio show host and professional psychic, Pamala Oslie also sees auras and has discovered that different aura colors reveal important information about you - your personality, life purpose, relationship style and best compatibilities, most fulfilling careers, best way to create money, strengths in raising children, potential health problems, and much more. Pamala has created a brief aura color quiz so that you can discover your own personal colors. Then you can discover more about yourself and how you can create your most fulfilling life by reading the descriptions and watching the videos about your colors.

Pam has also been speaking to people who have crossed over for almost three decades. She has been a popular guest speaker at IANDS - The International Association for Near Death Studies.

Pam appears on numerous TV and radio shows, has been a featured speaker at the 2012 TEDx Talks, Fortune 500 companies, the International Forum on New Science, Conscious Life Expo and in many national magazines. She has an international clientele and has also written many successful and popular books.

Staci Wells www.staciwells.com

Staci Wells has the unique ability to see our pre-birth planning sessions and hear the conversations we have with one another before we are born. Through a lifetime of communication with her Spirit Guides, Staci has a unique awareness of karma, pre-birth planning, and our soul's evolutionary progress. Her exceptional intuitive access to information allows her to pinpoint central life issues with laser-like precision. **With gentleness, kindness and loving compassion, Staci shines a fresh new light** on the deeper meaning of our planned life experiences. Her knowledge of metaphysics is wide-ranging, including in-depth experience as a gifted psychic medium, medical intuitive, numerologist and tarot reader

Marilyn Kapp has been channeling since age two after witnessing her Grandfather leave his body. For her it was normal to continue the relationship and all its love and fun.

With intention and life experience, Marilyn's ability expanded, providing a vehicle to those who have passed through with which they could express their emotions and concerns.

Often called "therapy on speed," Marilyn gently guides you through the process, providing an opportunity for healing as well as realizing and expanding your own channeling potential.

Marilyn is continually grateful to be a catalyst for healing.

You can contact Marilyn through her website, MarilynKapp.com, or by calling 760-602-0228.

HEREAFTER MUSICAL: For more information go to www.hereaftermusical.com

"Hereafter Musical" explores what happens when a loved one dies from the perspective of both the living AND the dead. Dealing with the universal theme of life and death, "Hereafter Musical" takes the audience on a special journey filled with tears, laughter and song. And by show's end, it delivers a sense of closure for both the characters AND the audience that is truly a unique and satisfying theatrical experience.

Made in the USA
Columbia, SC
15 September 2017